The Local Church in Ministry

WILLIAM M. PINSON, JR.

BROADMAN PRESS/Nashville, Tennessee

Library of Congress Catalog Card Number: 73-75629
Dewey Decimal Classification: 361.7
Printed in the United States of America

To
Bobbie, Meredith, and Allison Pinson
whose lives went into the
writing of this book

FOREWORD

A growing number of local churches are discovering new vitality through programs of ministry to the physical, social, and emotional needs of persons. Pastors, missionaries, and volunteer workers are serving fruitfully in a variety of creative ministries.

Churches bear witness to Christ and the Christian faith by such expressions of Christian love. In addition these ministries open doors of opportunity for verbal witness to the gospel.

There is much for all of us to learn from the experiences of other churches and other Christians, of both our own and other Christian denominations. A few years ago the Southern Baptist Home Mission Board, joined by the Convention's Christian Life Commission, sensed a need for a careful study of what churches of various faiths in different parts of the country were doing in ministry to human needs.

William M. Pinson, Jr., associate professor of Christian ethics, Southwestern Baptist Theological Seminary, Fort Worth, Texas, was engaged to do this study as his sabbatical leave project. Bringing to the effort a disciplined mind and a sensitive spirit, Dr. Pinson has produced in this book a comprehensive and relatively concise guidebook for churches' involvement in expanding their ministry to persons. We are grateful for the excellent and thorough work of Dr. Pinson.

It is my hope that this volume will provide needed insights and encouragement to hundreds of churches as they minister to the urgent needs of the people of their respective communities.

Arthur B. Rutledge
Executive Secretary-Treasurer
Home Mission Board, SBC

PREFACE

Acknowledging the assistance of all who made this book possible would take many pages. Hundreds of pastors, church staff personnel, church members, professors, and denominational executives gave generously of their time to help me. A few, however, played such significant roles that the book would have been impossible without them.

President Robert E. Naylor and the trustees of the Southwestern Baptist Theological Seminary granted me a fifteen-month study leave.

The Home Mission Board of the Southern Baptist Convention made possible the travel and writing. Dr. Arthur Rutledge graciously supported my proposal to study the ministry programs of the churches in the United States. Dr. Hugo Culpepper and Dr. Loyd Corder provided administrative supervision. E. Warren Rust guided the manuscript through to completion.

Cecil White, assistant librarian for public services of the Fleming Library of the Southwestern Baptist Theological Seminary, helped in many ways, particularly with bibliography.

Dr. Don Hammer, coordinator for the Urban Strategy Council of the Baptist General Convention of Texas, offered a number of suggestions to improve the manuscript.

Mrs. Don Hammer typed the manuscript several times as it assumed final form.

Bobbie, my wonderful wife, and Meredith and Allison, our delightful daughters, faithfully accompanied me on the travel and patiently endured the writing of the manuscript.

To all these I owe a very special thank you.

William M. Pinson, Jr.

CONTENTS

Retired Persons
Runaway Youth
School Dropouts
Sick
Single Adults
Slow Learners
Speech Handicap

Transition Neighborhood
  Residents
Unemployed
Unwed Parents
Widow and Widower
Working Mother
Youth

Adopt-a-Building Program
Adult Education Classes
After School Activities
Amigos
Art Festival
Arts, Crafts, Hobby Classes
Baby Sitting Co-op
Block Partners
Book Store
Breakfast for Preschool
  Children
Camping
Care for Dependent Persons
Charm and Grooming
  Classes
Child Care Near Employment
  Centers
Child Care Near Hospital
  District
Child Care—Short Term
Christian Bar
Christian Night Club
Christian Restaurant
Citizenship Classes
Classes in Domestic Skills
Clothing Center
Clubs
Coffeehouse
Community Center
Community Listening Teams
Community Study Groups
Companion Church Program
Consumer Skills Education
Craft Center
Credit Union
Counseling
Drama
Drug Prevention Center
Educational Ministry
Emergency Domestic Help

Employment Opportunities
English Classes
Family Life Program
Fellowship Groups
Financial Planning and Advice
Food Center
Form-Fill-out Assistance
Foster Home Care
Fund for Justice
Grief Therapy
Halfway Houses
Headliners
Health Education
Home Handyman Service
Homes for Runaway Youth
Hostel for Transient Youth
Hot Lunch Program
Housing Improvement
International Club
Kindergarten
Legal Aid
Library
Literacy Training
Loan Fund for Recently
  Released Prisoners
Mass Communication
Meal-on-Wheels Program
Medical and Dental Care
Mom's Day-Night Out
Multiple Ministries in
  Shopping Centers
Music
Neighborhood Improvement
  Organization
Newcomer Service
Personal Grooming for the
  Needy
Personnel Resource File
Planned Parenthood Clinic
Prenatal Care and Counsel

Preschool Program
Recreation
Recreation Clinics
Remedial Reading Program
Rent and Utility Assistance
Resort Leisure Ministry
Roving Street Minister
Scholarships for Youth from
    Poverty Areas
School for Excluded Children
Senior Citizens' Lounge
Sex Education Programs
Shopping for the Handicapped
Sisters Program
Small Group Foster Care
Sponsor Big Brother, Big
    Sister Programs
Staff Members for Ministry

Study Hall
Teen Center
Telephone Checkup Service
Telephone Counseling and
    Referral
Thrift Store
Town Hall Discussions
Training in Community
    Services
Training Program for Ministry
Transportation
Tutoring
Visitation of the Confined
Vocational Training
Weight Reducing and Exercize
    Programs
Youth Service Corps

INTRODUCTION

Should Christians minister to total human need—spiritual, physical, mental, social? The answer from the Bible is a clear yes.[1] Should churches care for the whole person? Again the answer is yes.[2] The Bible is shot through and through with explicit commands to help people who hurt or who are in difficulty. Outstanding churchmen of the past were aware of the biblical mandate to minister.[3] Many Christians today are attempting to follow the clear call from God to care for all aspects of human need. Driven by a Christlike compassion for people, churches are developing hundreds of ministry programs. Diverse as the congregations which gave them birth, these programs have one thing in common. They seek to bear witness to Christ's love for people.

The rapid increase in the number and variety of church efforts to meet human need signals a new advance. God's people in cities and hamlets are going on record that they care about others. No longer content merely to profess their faith, they put it into action. A few years ago numerous churches offered mainly preaching and Bible study. Many began to shrivel and die. Then the spark of Christian compassion exploded the capacity to care which exists among God's

---

[1] Basic to any study of a church's ministry is a clear understanding of ministry in the biblical framework. Space does not permit a detailed discussion, but I do suggest the following references:

Exodus 22:25-27
Leviticus 14:21-32; 19:1-18
Deuteronomy 15:1-11,19-21
Isaiah 1:1-31
Jeremiah 5:25-29
Ezekiel 18
Hosea 6:6
Amos 2:6; 5:11-12,24; 8:4-6
Micah 6:6-8
Matthew 4:4,23-24; 8:1-4,5-17; 9:1-10,27-38; 11:28-30; 12:9-14,22-24; 14:27-36; 15:21-38; 17:14-18; 23:1-33
Mark 2:1-12; 6:45-52; 7:24-37; 8:22-26; 10:46-52; 12:35-44

people. The churches looked out on the surrounding community and
saw need—all kinds of need. And the people of God went out on a
mission to meet that need. In hundreds of cases the total ministry
which resulted brought new life to the churches. Apparently multiple
ministry is a key for church growth in the future. It is certainly a
means of bearing witness for Christ.

These new developments stimulated my long-term interest in
evangelism, ethics, and church growth. On a fifteen-month study
leave, I lived in many areas of the United States. My purpose was
to find out what churches of all denominations were doing to meet
total human need. I discovered certain basic patterns and found

---

Luke 5:12-26; 7:1-17; 8:1-3,40-56; 15:11-19; 17:11-19; 18:15-17,35-43;
    19:1-10
John 4:1-25,46-53; 5:1-9; 9:13-16
Acts 3:1-10; 9:32-35; 14:8-10; 16:16-19
Romans 12:3-8,13; 15:5
1 Corinthians 13:3; 16:1-4
2 Corinthians 9:1-15
Galatians 6:10
Ephesians 4:11-16
1 Timothy 5:16; 6:18
2 Timothy 3:17
James 1:27; 2:15-16
1 John 3:17-18; 4:19-21

The following books set forth biblical bases for ministry: *The Diakonic Task*
(Atlanta: Home Mission Board, Southern Baptist Convention, 1970) by Walter
Delamarter; *The Greening of the Church* (Waco: Word Books, 1971) by
Findley B. Edge; *A Ringing Call to Mission* (New York: Abingdon Press,
1966) by Alan Walker.

[2]Insight into the church's ministry in the New Testament period is seen in
the following:
    Acts 2:45, 3:1-10; 4:32-35, 6:1-6; 8:7; 9:32-35; 14:8-10; 16:16-19; 26:16;
        28:7-15
    Romans 12:7; 15:25,27
    1 Corinthians 16:1-4
    2 Corinthians 1:4; 8:13-15; 9:1-15
    Ephesians 4:12
    Colossians 3:14
    1 Timothy 5:9-16
    2 Timothy 3:17
    1 Peter 4:11

[3]For a more detailed discussion see the following: *Twenty Centuries of
Great Preaching,* 13 vols. (Waco: Word Books, 1971) by Clyde E. Fant, Jr.
and William M. Pinson, Jr.; *Compassion and Community* (New York: Association Press, 1961) by Haskell M. Miller; *The Church and Social Welfare*
(Philadelphia: Westminster Press, 1962) by Alan Keith-Lucas.

hundreds of specific programs. I also learned that many churches were unaware of the new trend. This book is an effort to share what God is doing through total ministry in the churches of America. It is not the whole story. But it is a guide which hopefully will help churches witness through ministry.

The first section shares basic approaches for effective church ministry. The second sets forth suggested ministries and resources for meeting specific types of human need. The third section presents examples of programs. The fourth lists resources for ministry. Finally, an Appendix provides tools which many have found useful. Every effort has been made to insure accuracy. But in case of errors please notify the author so that corrections can be made in subsequent editions.

The first section deals with ministry in general terms. The discussions are not theoretical. I have reported what churches are doing, not what someone theorizes they ought to do. The two following sections also report church activity. What is described differs from the first section in being more specific. It is not more practical. Nothing could be more practical than general guidelines for a church in ministry.

To plunge right into the second and third sections without reading the first is a mistake. You can drown in a sea of possibilities before taking a single stroke to do anything. It is important to understand how specific activities fit into a general program of ministry. Only then can ministries be effectively initiated.

Observing a church in ministry is much more helpful than reading sketchy accounts of its programs. But examples of specific churches in ministry are absent from this book.[4] Space was one reason for the omission. The main factor was the rapid changes which take place in church programs. A church listed as conducting a certain program may drop it. The Home Mission Board of the Southern Baptist Convention is at present investigating the possibility of utilizing a computer to provide up-to-date examples of churches in specific ministries.

When true to their biblical mandate, churches are concerned about whole people. Most institutions are devoted only to certain aspects of human life, not to wholeness. Some care about physical needs,

[4]See Section IV for books which describe ministry programs in individual churches.

others about emotional, and many about social. The people of God bring to caring the plus of spiritual concern. They also devote themselves to Christ's lordship over all dimensions of human life. If we follow Jesus, we will not overlook any dimension. This book is an effort to help us minister effectively to the glory of God by bringing the whole gospel to bear on the total person in the entire community.

Programs alone are inadequate. Only the power of God can give life. Vitality in ministry comes from God's working through his people yielded to his will. All the words in this book will be as the valley of dry bones unless the Spirit of God breathes on them. Then they shall live, and churches will be brought to new life.

I

A Plan for Ministry

Ministry by churches is nothing new. Although great churches have always cared for total human need, few have had a comprehensive plan for ministry. Such plans are now being developed. Out of the experiences of hundreds of congregations in ministry a number of helpful guidelines have emerged. The following suggestions can be applied to all types of churches—large and small, urban and rural, wealthy and poor, new and old.

Basic Approach

Each congregation must hammer out its own approach. But the following principles are followed by most churches in effective ministry programs.

Care for the total person.—A Christian approach to ministry demands concern for the total person. Efforts should be made to meet all human need—mental, emotional, physical, and spiritual. To feed and clothe a person but fail to tell him of Christ's transforming power is to cheat him. To feed and clothe him only to gain an opportunity to preach to him is to disillusion him. It is not a matter of evangelism versus social ministry. It is a matter of caring for total human need—and that calls for evangelism *and* social ministry.

Be unapologetically Christian.—A church's ministry should not be merely a humanitarian project. It should be distinctly Christian. The motivation is the love of God in Christ. The goal is to bring men to wholeness through Christ. Thus a Christian ministry has a spiritual plus which non-Christian ministries do not have. This plus factor should be emphasized not hidden. If a church fails to make clear the spiritual dimension of its concern, an unbeliever can conclude one of two things. The church really does not believe what it says about God in Christ, or the church is being deceitful and will spring the spiritual trap after it gets people involved. It is best to be honest and straightforward from the beginning. People should under-

17

stand they don't have to become Christians to get help. They should also realize they will receive a Christian witness. At times there may be no opportunity to present the Christian message. Certainly these should be considered exceptions rather than the rule.

Minister with a community, not in it or to it.—A church should not go about its ministry with a paternalistic air. Persons in a community should be consulted about what they feel should be done. A church must communicate a desire to work *with* people in dealing with the problems *they* feel are significant. Beware of becoming more concerned about developing a program than meeting need. It is a common pitfall.

Help people to help themselves.—The intent of ministry should be to help persons help themselves. Some persons are by circumstance dependent—the retarded, the senile, the mentally ill, for example. But most people can become independent. Many needy people have little sense of personal worth. They feel unwanted and useless. Consequently they often act in a repulsive, irresponsible way. Such people need to develop a feeling of personal worth. A ministry program can help supply this need. Treat each person with respect. Afford an opportunity for those receiving ministry to minister to others.

Undertake only what can be done well.—If a church promises more than it can fulfil, the result will be disillusionment. If it initiates more than can be carried through, frustration and resentment will develop. Future ministries will be very difficult to start. People in the community will regard promises with skepticism. It is better to do a few things well than many poorly. A church should strain its resources to do all it can but refuse to overextend itself. Since most churches face more need than can possibly be met, determining priorities is highly important.

Major on people more than program design.—If the right kind of people can be enlisted for leadership, they will develop adequate plans for ministry. Without responsible, creative leadership even the most brilliantly designed programs will fail. More important than buildings, equipment, or program design are the people who lead. Developing mature Christians with a clear sense of mission is a top priority for all churches.

Prepare for difficulties.—Problems and difficulties are encountered in most ministries. Persons in need sometimes reject those who try to help them. Many will fail to respond. They are suspicious or hostile. Some will try to take advantage of those who seek to help them. There will be disappointment and genuine heartache. Controversy may erupt. If people approach ministry realistically, prepared to deal with conflict and accept disappointment, they are more likely to do an effective job.

Be flexible and innovative:—No plan should be considered fixed and unchangeable. Because both churches and communities are constantly in flux, a plan of ministry must be flexible. It should be adjusted to meet new needs. Innovation and experiment are essential. The organization for ministry should not be some prepackaged, ready-made import from another church or a denominational office. Valuable ideas and insights can be gained from others, but a plan should be designed specifically for a particular church.

A plan should provide for ministry to all types of needs and to all kinds of people. If the ministry follows the biblical example, no one will be excluded because of race, creed, or economic condition. Black and white, rich and poor, citizen and alien, young and old—all are to be included. No human need should be considered off limits for the church.

Ministry can include simple individual acts and vast corporate planning. Individuals should be equipped to minister at work, in school, in their neighborhood, in social activity—wherever they are. Small groups, committees, and task forces can render effective ministries. Large corporations, boards, and agencies may be necessary for certain programs. The form of the organization should be dictated by the function it performs. It is better to build a structure around specific needs rather than develop an organization and then go in search of needs.

Prevent as well as correct.—It is important both to help persons who hurt and to correct the social problems which hurt them. Most churches major on caring for the victims of social problems rather than correcting the problems. But both tasks are important. For example, a church which has a ministry for tutoring slow learners should also consider doing something about substandard housing, malnutrition, inadequate medical care, and racism—all of which tend to cause children to be slow learners. An adequate plan of ministry will deal not only with symptoms but also with causes.

Ways to Begin

Churches have initiated effective ministries in various ways. No single way works best. The resources of the church, including its finances, facilities, organizations, and personnel and the nature of the community determine to a large degree what approaches may be taken.

Altered circumstances frequently trigger an expanded plan of ministries—a change of neighborhood from middle to low income, an influx of ethnic minorities, or the arrival of a new pastor are common factors. In other cases ministries develop as spontaneous response to need. Some emerge from small groups in prayer, Bible study, and fellowship. But more often they result from planning and motivation provided by missionary organizations in the church. In the latter case lay people led the way, but pastoral encouragement and support strengthened the work and lack of pastoral support severely crippled it.

Possible Approaches

There are two basic ways to develop a plan of ministry. Either can be effective. Both are found in a variety of forms. The first is a self-study approach. It deals with the church program as a whole, not with ministry alone. It is concerned with church renewal, self-analysis, and theology. It relates with all aspects of a church's life—worship, education, evangelism, as well as ministry. An effort is made to lead the church to view itself as a servant church, to be open to new approaches, and to cast free from unfruitful traditions. The church council, composed of the leaders of church organizations, or a special committee can evaluate the church and make recommendations for changes. The church council or special committee should: (a) define the goals of the church in the light of the biblical revelation; (b) describe the needs of the community; (c) evaluate how well the church is achieving its goals and meeting the needs; (d) determine what changes should be made; (e) present recommendations to the congregation. Church members should be led in discussions of the questions considered in the evaluation.

For those interested primarily in ministry action the self-study approach has significant drawbacks. It can bog down in a wasteland of words while crying needs go unmet. It can lead to unnecessary theological division among the members. An alternate way is to plunge into ministry action without going through a self-study or establishing a theological rationale. In the second basic approach use the organizations in the church to begin meeting obvious needs in the community. In addition, a survey can be made to locate other needs.

Such an approach has several points in its favor. People usually learn more by doing than by talking. Goals for specific action can be more clearly defined than those for self-study or renewal; as a result people are more easily motivated and less frustrated. There is likely to be more agreement on concrete acts to meet human need than on the theological basis for such acts. There is less chance of bogging down in endless discussion. Action produces results and encourages more action. People are more likely to be changed by involvement in ministry programs than by committee meetings and discussions.

Suggestions for Developing the Ministry

For most churches developing extensive ministries involves a major change in the life of the congregation. Whoever presents such a plan needs to make a careful appeal. Usually the pastor, a layman, or group of lay people will lead. The following suggestions apply directly to the person or groups who are leading but can be used by anyone.

Maintain good relations.—Without a good relationship between leader and people, little can be accomplished. The people must feel that a leader is a responsible, trustworthy person who desires their best interests. Spiritual maturity, sound business practice, and integrity are essential. As an example, a man who has been pastor of a church for many years and has built up a reservoir of good will can often move quickly in innovative programs. But a new pastor usually comes to a church with the good will of the people and can also begin these programs. The key to success is not how long a pastor has been in a church but his attitude and ability.

Be positive.—Stress what *can* be done and what opportunities are available. Praise existing ministries and assume the people will want to continue to expand their outreach. Don't emphasize past failure to minister, ridicule present efforts, scold the people for inactivity, or display a gift for sarcasm. Such efforts will only win resistance.

Point out the relationship of evangelism and ministry.—Evangelism and ministry go hand in hand. A church exists to bear witness to

Jesus Christ. The purpose of witness is to lead people to respond to God's invitation to new life in Christ. This witness is carried out in three primary ways: (1) Proclamation of the good news that God was in Christ reconciling the world unto himself. (2) Christian fellowship as a foretaste of what God has in store for those who accept his reconciling love. (3) Ministry as an expression of the nature of the new life in Christ. In a sense, ministry and the fellowship of Christian love validate the proclaimed message. They can win a hearing from a skeptical world.

Ministry brings persons into contact with the gospel who otherwise would not be touched. Most Christians live within a narrow limit of personal relations. They are with people of similar interests, economic standing, social status, and skin color. Aside from casual contacts, the average person encounters the same limited number of people each week. If new evangelistic opportunities are to develop, a Christian must break this pattern. One way to do this is through door-to-door visitation. Another is by ministry.

Ministry relates Christians to persons they would not otherwise know. The contact is made within the framework of loving concern. There is no better circumstance in which to share the good news than this. Ministry leads the way to proclamation. The Christian doesn't use ministry as bait to trap a person into listening to a sermon. Rather he cares about total human need.

Relate ministry to survival needs.—A few church leaders seem to glory in numerical decline as evidence of faithfulness to God's will. Their attitude is, "We must be succeeding as a church because we are dying as an institution." Such an outlook forgets institutions are a necessary part of life. It is also shortsighted. If a church dies serving the world there will be no more service from that church. Sustaining the church as an institution is a valid Christian concern. Maintaining the institution is not an end in itself, but the institution can be a means to the end of Christian witness. Apart from the institutional expression of the Christian faith many ministries could not be performed.

Any institution—including a church—needs members, finances, and facilities. Ministry programs can help maintain all three. Many Christians feel churches have not done what they should in ministry. A number have become involved in nonchurch efforts to meet human need while also remaining active in a church. Others have forsaken the church for secular ministry programs. Young people in particular want churches to be more active in caring for the hurt of society. A church which engages actively in ministry programs is more likely to attract and hold these ministry-oriented Christians than one which does not. It offers channels of service other than teaching or singing.

Persons interested in caring for total human need will also tend to be generous in giving to a church with a well-developed program of ministry. If a church does not lessen its zeal for evangelism, education, and missions while adding a dimension of ministry, it should strengthen its financial picture.

Facilities can be more easily justified when they are fully utilized rather than slightly used. In ministry programs buildings and equipment often can be kept in service seven days a week and sometimes twenty-four hours a day. Such efficient use of facilities encourages support of building programs and purchase of equipment.

Ministry is only one aspect of church growth. Ministry apart from effective preaching, personal visitation, stimulating Bible study, and pastoral care will not be sufficient to maintain growth in a church. On the other hand, a church, even when growing rapidly in membership, finances, and facilities, is not what it ought to be if it lacks a dynamic ministry to total human need.

Stress a connection with the past as well as the challenge of the new.—Some churchmen are by nature suspicious of innovation and comfortable with tradition. Help these to realize that ministries are in keeping with, not a departure from, the best in Christian tradition. Other churchmen like to be part of the new and creative. They tend to be critical of traditional approaches. Point these to fresh methods of ministry. Challenge them to be part of innovative programs to help people.

Use church program organizations.—Missionary organizations in the church and the Sunday School are units of the church organization that quite naturally perform ministry tasks for the church. Make full use of these organizations in assigning responsibilities for ministry. Southern Baptists, for example, have been stressing the involvement of churches in ministry with the Sunday School taking the lead in ministering to persons in the church family and the missionary organizations taking the lead in ministering to persons beyond the church family in a variety of mission action. Sunday School, Woman's Missionary Union, and Brotherhood have a plan for enlistment.

motivation, placement, and training of persons doing ministry and mission action.

Avoid a one-sided approach.—A church cannot build its entire life around ministry. In themselves they will not sustain membership and finances. Aggressive programs of visitation, enlistment, evangelism, and stewardship are also necessary. Many people are attracted to a church for what they can receive, not for what they can contribute. Some are substandard Christians, but many are hurt people needing help. They should be welcomed. Through nurture most will grow into serving maturity in Christ. But worship, fellowship, and Christian education are essential in a church if such growth is to take place.

A church should avoid putting all of its energy into ministering to people outside the church or dealing with social problems. People within the church often need help as much as those on the outside. Prophetic preaching on social issues is important, but so also is preaching to comfort and guide individual Christians. People need to be assured the pastor will not forget them in his zeal to minister to the community. Without this assurance, many will not enthusiastically support a plan of ministry.

Show that ministry aids spiritual growth.—Worship and Bible study alone are not adequate for healthy spiritual growth. In fact, they can be selfish acts which stunt growth in Christ. Christian service coupled with worship and Bible study provides an excellent combination for spiritual development. A person encountering and dealing with desperate human need soon discovers the limits of his own resources. He learns to tap spiritual reserves and claim the promises of God to strengthen those who call on him. Thus in ministering to others the Christian is often helped to mature spiritually.

Answer objections considerately.—The Bible clearly teaches caring for the needs of others. Jesus set an example of ministry which the early church followed. In the light of these facts, why do many churches lack an aggressive involvement ministry? Part of the answer rests in ignorance; some people simply are not aware of the needs of others. Apathy is another factor; many who know about human problems don't care enough to do anything. Strangely enough, some Christians actively oppose ministry programs in local churches. Their objections need to be carefully answered.

Some churchmen insist ministry is unnecessary. They believe when a person becomes a Christian his problems are solved; God will take care of his every need. Therefore, the argument goes, since conversion meets both temporal and eternal needs, the church should spend all of its time in evangelism. The Bible does not teach that becoming a Christian solves all one's problems. The early church cared for sick and needy Christians. Furthermore, Jesus did not spend all of his time in verbal efforts to win followers. A large portion of his time was given for ministry to total need—spiritual, physical, mental, and emotional.

Some suggest ministry takes away from evangelism. Since they believe evangelism is the basic function of a church, ministry is viewed as a handicap. Such as view failes to see the close relation between evangelism and ministry. A church without ministry is not as evangelistic as it could be.

Some oppose ministry because they feel it is an expression of the social gospel, a merely humanitarian program lacking an emphasis on personal conversion. Activities by a church which have a purely humanitarian rationale should be opposed. Church programs which stress social change apart from individual conversion are sub-Christian. But effective ministry is neither merely humanitarian nor purely social. It emphasizes spiritual factors and the need for personal salvation.

Another common argument against ministry is that other institutions have ministries to meet physical, mental, and emotional needs. But only churches care for the spiritual. Churches should, therefore, major on what they alone are commissioned to do. Churches which are true to their calling as the body of Christ have no alternative, however, but to minister to the total needs of men. Furthermore, most communities have unmet needs. Also, churches in their total concern for men have a plus factor which most other groups lack—a spiritual dimension. Churches should do a better job of dealing with problems because of this.

Some argue that churches which become involved in ministry cease to grow. This is not true. Some churches active in ministry have experienced decline. But in most cases the ministry did not contribute to the loss. It impeded it. Other churches with multiple ministries have experienced growth—much of it attributable to the ministries. No single factor causes church growth or decline. The causes are complex. But ministry is far more likely to lead to church growth than to decline.

Some contend ministry plans and staff members are sometimes the cause of dissension. But few advocate doing away with them. Ministry is as essential as buildings and staff. It is invalid to oppose ministry because of possible controversy. Controversy is likely to erupt over any issue which people care deeply about and disagree on. Efforts in ministry are not immune to conflict. Ministries are especially likely to erupt in controversy when they threaten vested interests or stir prejudice. Efforts to provide decent housing may stir the wrath of slum landlords in a church. Or ministries for black children in a segregated congregation may run into opposition from racist church members. In such cases the lack of spiritual maturity in church members is demonstrated, not the undesirability of ministry.

Church staff members sometimes protest they are unable to fill all the present leadership positions in the church and don't want to develop more programs. Ministry is a vital part of the educational program. Furthermore, enlistment for ministry may not be as difficult as some fear. Many who feel they have no gift for teaching or who are deeply interested in ministry may respond quickly to the challenge. In light of the high priority given ministry in the life and teachings of Jesus and the New Testament churches, pastor and staff should give it high priority also. Making a place for ministry in an already full schedule may require giving up other less important tasks. Since those who need ministry are seldom in a position to push their cause, it is easy to give attention to more pressing demands. But pastor and staff should not overlook the needs of any.

Utilize a variety of methods to educate and motivate people.—Preaching, books, study groups, church conferences, retreats, ministry fairs,[1] and reports on the ministries of other churches all can be used. A very effective approach is to work with a small group of leaders motivating them to concern about total ministry. These persons can then serve as the nucleus of the church's effort to meet human need.

Emphasize the biblical basis for ministry.—An appeal to expand the church's ministry to the community should be based on the Bible. Most church members respect the authority of the Bible. They

---

[1]In such a fair booths are set up—in classrooms, a gym, halls, or wherever space is available—to display community needs and organizations seeking to meet the needs. As church members go from booth to booth, they learn about ministry possibilities. People can enlist to work in the area about which they feel most concerned.

are more likely to back ministries which are clearly biblical than those which are not. The Bible stresses that the people of God are to be a ministering people. This emphasis should be presented often in sermons, Bible studies, and articles.

Find the answers to basic questions.—Answers to the following must be found if an effective plan is to be developed:

What are the unmet needs in our community?

What resources do we have to meet these needs?

In light of the needs and our resources, which needs should we undertake to meet first?

What organizations in the church can most appropriately meet these needs?

Who should serve in these ministries? What skills do we need? How many persons do we need? How can the people who will serve in the ministries be trained?

What facilities will be needed?

How should the ministries be financed?

In what ways should the ministries be related to community agencies and other churches?

When and where do we begin?

How should we publicize the ministries?

In light of our experience with the operation of the ministry, what changes should be made to improve it? Is it worth continuing?

The following sections suggest ways to find answers to these and related questions.

Determining Needs

Determining which needs a church should try to meet calls for at least four steps: (1) Sensitize church members to be aware of human hurt. (2) Find specific needs in the community and learn what is being done about them. (3) Discover available resources for ministry. (4) Establish priorities for action.

Sensitize People

Adequate ministry depends on people sensitive to need. An insensitive person can confront a situation and never identify it as an opportunity for ministry. People unaware of problems are not likely to be concerned about ministry. A church member sensitive to human hurt will want to do something to help. Here are some ways to develop sensitivity.

Bible study on common human problems, such as poverty, hunger, crime, loneliness, family disorder, divorce, homosexuality, and sickness can help build awareness. So can prayer. When people ask God to make them more sensitive to human need, share with one another the specific problems they have encountered, and discuss possible ways to minister, they notice needs others fail to see. Study about current conditions can help make people more aware of human hurt. Preaching which presents both biblical truth and contemporary issues leads to greater sensitivity.

Find Specific Needs

Basic to any ministry is determining the specific needs in a community. Needs can be located in several ways.

General knowledge.—Caring persons who have lived in a community for a long time are usually aware of many unmet needs. These people will be able to list a number of possible ministries. Acts of ministry often lead to discovery of new needs. When people encounter ministry opportunities, they should report them to persons responsible for church ministry programs. A church well-known for compassion is sought by people in trouble.

Surveys.—In most communities a survey of human need will prove helpful. Such a survey calls for a systematic analysis of a community. The lists of needs and possible ministries in sections II and III of this book can serve as a guide for a survey. Surveys can be conducted by professionals, such as sociologists or social workers, or by average church members. Professionals usually do a more thorough study and prepare a more detailed report than persons untrained in analyzing social issues. A survey conducted by church members, however, has the advantage of exposing them directly to problems in the community. Thus they are motivated to minister while they locate needs.

Surveys can be carried out in a number of ways. Some excellent suggestions on making surveys are provided by denominational agencies in survey guides or workbooks. Some such resources are listed in Section IV. Alert, sensitive Christians can walk or ride through the community noting needs and ministry possibilities. They can interview government officials, schoolteachers and administrators, business and labor leaders, welfare workers, and staff members of community help agencies. They can study census statistics and information available from city planners related to such matters as housing, education, and income levels. An adequate survey seeks to discover answers to three questions: (1) What are the human needs in our community? (2) What is being done to meet these needs? (3) What needs are being inadequately dealt with? Answers to these questions help a church determine what programs to develop.

Headliners.—Some churches discover needs by scanning newspapers for stories about human tragedy—a home destroyed by fire, a father killed or injured, a small business destroyed by flood. Human interest stories often provide leads for ministry. Several churches have formed groups, frequently known as Headliners, to read papers and contact responsible ministry groups in the church about the needs they discover.

Discover Resources

Resources consist primarily of people, organizations, finances, and facilities. Those guiding the development of the ministries should seek answers to questions such as these: What are the experiences, talents, skills, and training of people in our church which equip them for ministry? Which persons in the community who are not members of the church could be enlisted to help? What church program organizations have been assigned or can be assigned responsibility for ministry? In what ways can the church's property, buildings, and equipment be used for ministry? What other facilities can be used for ministry?

Establish Priorities

Likely a church will find it impossible to meet all the needs discovered. The following questions are helpful in determining which should have priority: Which problems affect the most people in our community? Which are the most severely damaging? Which are being dealt with in the least adequate way? Which are we the best equipped to handle in light of our resources in facilities and personnel? Which do we feel the Holy Spirit is leading us to deal with?

Those responsible for developing a program of ministry should list the problems or needs which answer each question. Those listed most frequently should probably receive priority attention. But such decisions cannot be made on the basis of reason alone. Prayer and the leadership of the Holy Spirit will help determine priorities.

Developing an Organization

No single pattern of organization will work in every church. Each must devise its own approach according to size, location, resources, and opportunities. Each will follow its own denominational plan.

In relation to the church, ministries fall into the following basic categories: (1) Ministries performed by units within the church, such as missionary organizations or Sunday School classes; (2) Individual members helping others in and through their vocation, family, social activity, and community service.

Ministry groups can be organized around different functions or interests. (1) *Issues,* such as low-cost housing, poverty, racism, and alcohol control, can be the basis of a ministry group. The people involved devise programs to deal with the issues. (2) *Personal needs* and problems, such as illiteracy, mental illness, mental retardation, unemployment, and drug addiction, can result in ministry groups being developed. (3) *Geographic areas,* such as a transition neighborhood, an inner city, or an apartment house complex, can be the center of a ministry effort. (4) *Age groups,* such as infants, children, youth, and the aged, may have special groups formed around them to devise ministries. (5) *Special programs,* such as counseling, recreation, medical care, and coffeehouse, or a telephone referral service, often require ministry groups.

Ministry groups will be of two basic types according to duration— short term and ongoing. Certain ministries may require only a short-term effort—a summer recreation program for inner-city young people or emergency measures for flood relief. When the project is completed, the group directing it is dissolved. Most ministry efforts will be continuing. They require assignment of responsibility to action groups or task forces. A separate action group for each ministry is usually more effective than one committee responsible for all programs.

A Group Functioning

A ministry group sometimes forms spontaneously in response to a need. A prayer or study group may feel compelled to act when confronted by a problem, such as increasing narcotic addiction in a community. In other cases a need is discovered by the pastor or another church member and a group is established to deal with it. A ministry group will need to take the following steps.

(1) *Understand the need.*—This requires study, consultation with experts, and firsthand exposure to the problem.

(2) *Develop a plan.*—On the basis of an understanding of the problem the group can develop a plan of action. In devising a plan the following questions should be considered: What resources in the community are available to help meet this particular need? How can we utilize them? What facilities will we need? How can we obtain them? What will it cost? How can we finance it? How many people will we need? How can we enlist them? What special skills are required? Where can we secure persons with the skills? How can we train others?

(3) *Act.*—The plan should be put into action as soon as possible. Careful preparation is essential but the group should *not* wait until they have developed a perfect plan. If they do, they will never act. A problem cannot be adequately understood until people are dealing with it. A plan cannot be refined until it is in operation. Skills are not developed until they are applied. Many groups exhaust themselves preparing and never act. Talk can become a substitute for ministry.

(4) *Review and revise.*—Periodically the group should review the program, evaluate its effectiveness, and determine what changes should be made.

Coordination of Ministries

In most churches many different groups are active in helping people. Men and women's organizations, youth organizations, and Sunday School classes frequently engage in ministry. Coordination of these diverse efforts can help the church be more effective in meeting human need. The ministry function should not be organized and centralized to the degree it stifles individual initiative, however. Several effective approaches can be used to coordinate ministry programs in a church.

Church Council.—The ministry function of a church is very important, and coordination of the activities of different groups in a single ministry plan is essential to its success. Coordination can perhaps best be done by the church council, under the leadership of the pastor. In the council, church leaders can agree on assignment of responsibilities and integrate the ministry plan in the total program of the church. Also, serving with the church council may be a church missions committee that can identify some needs which can be met by the church and can accept responsibility for some assignments which may involve providing facilities and employed personnel.

Pastor.—The pastor often serves as the coordinator and director of ministries. He is the natural leader and is aware of many unmet needs. He should not do the work alone. His task is primarily enlisting and training others for ministry.

Minister of education.—The minister of education under the leadership of the pastor usually coordinates the activities of the church program organizations, of which ministry is a vital part.

Director of ministries.—In large churches a full-time staff member may be utilized to coordinate and direct the ministry programs. His training should include both theology and social work. When a full-time staff member is not available or the church cannot afford one, a part-time staff member can be employed. Seminary students, graduate students in social work, social workers, teachers, and professors are often qualified and interested in such work.

Ministry Beyond the Normal Local Church Structure

The organizational structure described up to this point is within the framework of the typical local church. This is the most common approach to ministry and in many ways is the most effective. However, it is by no means the only approach. Ministry can be related to a local church in several ways. (See "Cooperating with Others.")

Some churches establish a separate organization for carrying out ministry. This is usually a distinct legal entity from the local church even though it often has the same staff members, is supported by the church, and uses the same facilities. It may carry a separate name. Often a full-time director guides the program. Such an arrangement is most often found in areas of concentrated need. It is sometimes financed in part by a denominational mission board.[2]

There are advantages in such an arrangement. It can be more flexible and innovative than many local church programs. It can reach people who would be repulsed by the usual church activities.

---

[2]See Guidelines for Communities-in-Crisis Projects (Division of Associational Services, Home Mission Board, SBC, Atlanta).

Its ministry program can be coordinated with the work of public and private welfare agencies more easily than a local church program can be.

Another approach is for ministry to be an integral part of a local church but carried out in scattered locations. Ideally, each ministry location should be in an area of distinct need and minister to that need with the support of the entire church. For example, a church might have meeting places and ministries in the inner city, in a plush suburb, in a transition community, and at a resort lake. Each location develops the ministries needed there. The names of the locations can indicate unity in diversity. For example, the First Baptist Church in Lakeview, the First Baptist Church in Park Place, the First Baptist Church in Centertown, the First Baptist Church-Downtown. Each location might have a separate pastor, or one pastor might serve several locations. Personnel and money are shared among the various locations. On certain occasions the entire church meets together for fellowship and worship. The staff serves all the church, but some staff members may have heavier responsibility at one location than at others.

At least two features distinguish this plan from the traditional one of a church establishing missions or new churches. The locations are not expected to become separate churches. This approach would not take the place of establishing new, separate churches. The locations are selected primarily on the basis of ministry opportunities. Such a structure will not work in every situation. But it is worth considering for several reasons. It enables people with great resources to share with those who have less—within the same fellowship. It can build strong witness and ministry points in areas of a city which would normally be unable to support such work. It can bring together persons from many different races, backgrounds, income patterns, and levels of education in one church fellowship.

A similar approach is for a church to establish and support missions or extension centers in areas of concentrated need. The mother church helps staff and finance ministry programs which otherwise would be impossible. The chief drawback is that too often the program is a ministry *to* a community rather than *with* it.

Some churches establish separate organizations for specific ministries. A halfway house for released prisoners, a drug prevention and rehabilitation center, a haven for girls newly arrived in a city, or a home for alcoholic women are examples of ministries which may require a separate, specialized organization. Frequently such ministries require full-time staff. For some ministries it is wise for the church to support part of the trustees or board of directors and the community part. Enlisting community involvement helps gain community support.

Securing Personnel

People are the most important part of ministry. Major on personnel. Secure dedicated, sensitive persons who are skilled in ministry and they will develop an effective organization. Enlisting the right persons for specific tasks is the key.

Sources

Any responsible person is a potential member of a ministry team. The age, temperament, and skills of a person will qualify him for some tasks more than for others. But there is a place for practically everyone. Most churches have several rich sources for ministry personnel. Among these are the missions organizations. Persons active in such organizations have usually been exposed to the biblical concept of meeting total need. In many churches they already carry the main load in ministry.

Youth groups can supply enthusiastic, hard working helpers. Often highly idealistic and altruistic, young people add much to a ministry team. Even children can help in some projects. Youth in special denominational programs can be a valuable part of a church ministry operation. Contact denominational agencies related to youth about securing student helpers. College students during school terms can also assist. Frequently campus Christian organizations channel large numbers of students into church ministry programs.

Social workers are often eager to use their professional training in a distinctly Christian way. They can not only provide counsel and training but also staff some of the ministry programs. Other professional persons, while busy, are frequently willing to contribute their services in Christian ministry. Teachers, dentists, physicians, nurses, pharmacists, lawyers, psychiatrists, psychologists, musicians, artists, actors, and many others can play a big part in church-related ministry. Others with special skills can be helpful. For example, carpenters, plumbers, painters, and electricians can construct ministry facilities. Cooks, seamstresses, and dietitians can teach homemaking. Accountants, lawyers, bankers, and other business-related persons can give counsel on finance. Mechanics, draftsmen, and secretaries can provide vocational training. Hairdressers, barbers, and beauticians can contribute services to the aged and poor.

People who have retired often have time, skills, and experience to give in ministry. Many senior citizens should be on the giving, not the receiving, end of ministry programs. Retired persons with skills in ministry can be added to church staffs at little cost since most of them already have income.

Home Bible study, prayer, and fellowship groups, increasingly numerous in churches, can provide sensitive, spiritual, deeply motivated persons for ministry. These groups sometimes become the nucleus of effective ministry programs.

Your church may not have anyone with the skills needed for a particular ministry. Such persons can be found in other churches. A regional organization to match those available for ministry with churches in need of specific skills is a valuable part of a total ministry program.

Enlistment

The enlistment of personnel is a many-faceted task. The organization responsible for the ministry will usually enlist people for new ministries. Groups frequently enlist the members needed for their work. A survey of church members to determine interests and skills is very helpful. The survey should be designed to secure information on vocation, working hours, special skills, hobbies, and ministry interests. (See Appendix C for sample survey form.) The results of the survey should be tabulated and used in enlistment. In large churches this information lends itself to computer storage. A survey of each new member should also be made. In the new members' orientation classes ministry programs can be presented.

Motivation

Motivation is vital to ministry. Serving Christ and others in love is the basic motive. Most people must be encouraged to keep at their task. There are several ways to do this. Bible study, prayer, and fellowship ought to be part of each ministry group. Members can covenant to pray for each other daily. Testimonies about experiences encourage continued ministry. As people share both victory and defeat, they grow closer. The sharing may take place mainly within the group. Testimonies can also be given in worship services, church fellowships, prayer meetings, or the church paper. Combined meetings of the various ministry groups provide an opportunity for all involved to learn what others are doing. Banquets and special recognition for those in ministries show that the church believes they are doing something important. Sermons on ministry indicate the pastor believes meeting total need is significant.

Placement

The placement of persons in a program is very important. It calls for a prayerful, thoughtful approach. In some cases, of course, placement just happens. A person becomes concerned about a need and goes to work to meet it. Or a particular ministry group attracts someone's interest and he asks to be a part. But generally people must be enlisted and properly placed if ministry is to reach its full potential.

Interests will play a key role. Most people tackle tasks they are interested in with greater enthusiasm than those they care little about. A ministry survey form for church members should include a section on interests and hobbies. Having this information will help match interests with tasks. Skills are another factor in placement. Certain tasks require special training or experience. Many are eager to relate vocational skills to church ministry programs. Carefully matching skills with needs cuts down on the training required for ministry. Use doctors and nurses in clinics, teachers in tutoring, and carpenters in renovating houses.

Possibility of success is also to be considered in placement. Persons newly enlisted or those easily discouraged should be given tasks where the success possibilities are high. Ministries where success is seldom experienced should be reserved for those who are experienced, stable, and emotionally mature. Personality and health are important too. Some people are naturals for certain jobs but misfits in others. Some thrive on hard manual labor while others can do only quiet tasks. People who are easily depressed should not be assigned to gruesome, painful situations. Daily schedule is another significant factor. A person's work and family life will determine to a great degree what ministries he can be involved in.

Conviction is perhaps the key factor. A person should feel that he is doing God's will, serving where he ought to be. Such conviction helps keep an individual at a task when it is difficult, frustrating, or boring.

Training

Persons enlisted and placed need to be trained for their task. Equipping ministry personnel is a continuing task. As much training should be given ministry leaders as is given those who teach in the Bible school or sing in the choir. Some persons already have the skills they need. But most will require training.

Training in ministry can be made part of the regular church educational program. Church organizations assigned responsibility for ministry can provide the necessary training of action groups or task forces. Several churches can cooperate in specialized training sessions. Special schooling may be required to develop certain skills. An individual or the church can pay the cost for such training as remedial reading, speech therapy, or work with the mentally retarded.

College and seminary professors, public-school teachers, social workers, counselors, staff members of welfare and service agencies, and other persons with special skills are often available to train church members for ministry. In some cases a church should offer and expect to pay for these services. Denominational staff members can help in some situations. Other churches with functioning plans of ministry can assist. By observing and working alongside persons involved in ministry, an individual can learn a great deal in a short time. Ministry groups in your church can train new members while they serve. In-service training is often the most effective kind.

How long should a person stay in the same ministry group? The answer depends on the person and the nature of the ministry. There are advantages to asking people to sign up for an extended period of time. A longer period of service enables persons to learn to minister effectively with the target group and it helps persons in the target group build up confidence and trust in those who minister.

For persons who do not desire to become committed for a long period of time, ministry projects are available. Special projects enable persons to use their skills and abilities in a shorter term of service. Also, short-term service prevents a group of people from feeling too possessive about a particular ministry.

Using Facilities and Equipment

Although a number of ministries can operate in a typical church building, others call for a separate place and special equipment. There are several options for ministry facilities.

Church Buildings

Many church buildings are already usable for ministries such as tutoring, citizenship classes, and clubs. With minor alterations they can be used for a wide variety of programs including clinics, recreation, and food centers. In constructing or remodeling church buildings, make them suitable for many different activities. Multipurpose buildings serve seven days a week in numerous ways.

Locating ministries in the church building has several advantages. It clearly identifies the church with the ministry. Normally it is the least expensive way to operate ministries. People become familiar with the church building through ministry and are more likely to come for Bible study and worship.

In some cases using church buildings may have disadvantages. It may cause non-Christians to avoid the program because of an aversion for churches. It may upset some church members to have people not of their own race, class, or degree of cleanliness in the buildings. It may require added maintenance expense with no corresponding increase in income.

A church with buildings in different locations (such as a church with missions or a church following the concept of one church in several different locations) is uniquely equipped for ministry. By majoring on the ministries appropriate for each location a church can offer a number of services. For example, a building in an older neighborhood can be used for ministry to the aging; one in a slum area for literacy work, narcotic control, and clubs; one in a new, upper-class suburb for family conferences, counseling, and foster care for neglected children.

The buildings of other churches sometimes can be used for ministries. A church may be well located for certain ministries but not have the necessary personnel. Under such circumstances another church can provide part of the personnel, train others, and utilize the buildings. Another approach is for several churches in an area to coordinate a ministry program. Each church building is used for a particular ministry and all of the churches share responsibility for personnel and finance. (See the section "Cooperating with Others.")

Mobile Units

Mobile units provide inexpensive, versatile facilities for many ministries. Three types of units are generally available: (1) mobile homes which are easily moved but must be towed; (2) self-propelled mobile homes; (3) buildings on skids which can be moved by truck. Mobile units can be custom made for many purposes, such as medical clinics, school rooms, worship centers, or libraries. Some can be used for a variety of activities in the community.

Special Facilities

Facilities apart from the church buildings are required for some ministries—homes for alcoholic women, the aged, and unwed mothers; halfway houses for released prisoners; shops for job training; centers for work with the retarded and physically handicapped. Sometimes a church can use secular buildings during periods when they otherwise would be idle. For example at night public schools might be used for tutoring, literacy, or recreation, a garage for training in mechanical work, an office for secretarial training, a beauty college for charm classes or hair styling for the poor or aged.

Public Facilities

Public facilities are sometimes available for ministry. Schools, parks, camps, and community centers are possible locations for ministry. The church should pay all expenses involved to avoid using taxpayers' money or violating their religious freedom.

Homes

Private residences are suitable locations for ministries such as tutoring, literacy training, and teaching domestic skills. A house in a needy neighborhood is used by some churches as a ministry center. Sometimes the house is owned by members of the church. In other cases it is rented or purchased. Members of a ministry group can move in, become part of the neighborhood, and develop a program to meet needs. Other members of the group help those in the house. A similar approach can be taken with apartments.

Commercial Buildings

Space in a commercial building may be needed for a ministry. Normally this space must be rented. Some owners are willing to rent at a lower rate if the space is used for a nonprofit ministry program.

Here are examples of use of such facilities: an area in an office building or a shopping center for counseling; an apartment in a low-income apartment complex for a thrift store, emergency food and clothing supplies, and counseling; a store front in a city used for a book store, counseling center, Bible study, literacy training, job placement, and clubs.

Special Equipment

The equipment normally owned by a church—tables, chairs, chalk-boards, recreation items, a kitchen—is adequate for most ministries. Some require special equipment—books on record or tape for the blind, literacy materials, busses equipped with lifts for the handi-capped, medical clinics, for example. Much special equipment, such as "talking books" for the blind, is available at little or no cost from organizations devoted to meeting specific needs. When free resources are unavailable, a church should investigate other options— share, lease, rent, or purchase. The rental business is expanding rapidly and items infrequently used can often be rented more economically than purchased.

Financing the Ministries

Funds for ministry programs can be obtained from several sources. The following are among the most common.

Church budget.—Just as a church has items in the budget for education, it ought to include items for ministry. These will be included in the regular budget making process.

Church assistance.—Churches in an area of heavy need frequently are unable to finance an adequate ministry plan. Churches with greater financial resources may help sponsor ministries in these churches. For example, a wealthy suburban church can help an inner-city church in a slum. Such cooperation should be encouraged, especially in the cities. In some communities interdenominational organizations help support ministries in churches.

Denominational agency assistance.—Limited funds are available from national or local denominational agencies for certain types of ministry. These funds are usually reserved for churches with small resources located in areas of great need. Under certain circumstances loans are available to purchase buildings. Some money is available for salaries of persons engaged in ministry. Never begin a program assuming funds will be available from a denominational agency. Always have financial arrangements clearly understood and worked out in advance. Some denominations, particularly through their boards of home missions, have money for ministries of other groups. Normally these funds are for initiating new, experimental, non-sectarian ministries rather than maintaining existing programs.

Community contributions.—Certain ministries are of such nature they win community support. Recreation programs, after-school activity for children of working parents, narcotic prevention efforts, clothing centers, and medical clinics, for example, often find favor with both church members and non-Christians. Such ministries frequently receive funds, materials, and even volunteer workers from the community at large. Normally, large scale campaigns to solicit support should be avoided. The word-of-mouth, low-key approach is better. The best way to gain community support is to do such an outstanding job that people volunteer to help.

Charge for services.—A charge for service rendered is sometimes appropriate. Such charges not only help finance the ministries but also aid the person receiving assistance to maintain self-respect. In most cases these charges will by no means cover the entire cost of the program. Examples of ministries for which charges might be made include day care, medical service, clothing, arts and crafts, and meals-on-wheels.

Grants from foundations.—A number of foundations make grants to assist ministries to human need. Usually such grants go to non-sectarian, community-wide organizations. A church is more likely to get a grant from a local or regional foundation than from a national one. For assistance in locating foundations see *Understanding Foundations* by J. Richard Taft.

Government funds.—Money is available through certain government programs for dealing with human need. Most such funds are federal grants and loans. Grants are made primarily for research and programs; loans are for construction of facilities, such as low-cost housing or homes of the aged.

Using government funds for church ministry has several drawbacks. It involves a complex, time-consuming process. It restricts the religious activity in the facilities. In the case of loans, it results in a long-term liability. It can violate religious liberty and the separation of church and state. If government funds are used for a project,

certain procedures will help avoid serious problems. Establish a
separate corporation apart from the church to be responsible for
the project. Enlist members for the board of directors of the
corporation from the community who are not members of a church.

Cooperating with Others

A local church can strengthen its ministry by cooperating with
other churches and organizations. A church should not remain aloof
when numerous opportunities are available for cooperation. Cooperative ministry can take several forms.

Churches of the Same Denomination

Direct cooperation with other churches of the same denomination
is possible in most communities. At least five distinct relations are
possible.

Clusters.—Churches located near one another can coordinate their
ministry efforts to avoid overlap. This is sometimes referred to as
the "cluster concept." Those responsible for ministry from churches
in the same general area meet and discuss projects. They determine
which specific needs each church will care for. They might also agree
to share personnel and costs. This approach avoids the waste of
overlap. Instead of several churches in one area ministering to a
limited number of deaf, retarded, and handicapped persons, each
church can specialize.

Teams.—Two churches in different types of settings can join for
ministry. A wealthy suburban church and an inner-city church in
financial difficulty might form a team. Or a white and a black
congregation might team to minister and deal with the problem of
racism.

Separate organization.—Churches in an area can form a separate
organization for ministry. Such an organization normally requires a
paid staff member to coordinate activities. The expense is shared by
all the churches. Each also shares in supplying volunteer workers
and facilities. A separate organization for ministry may require a
separate facility, something like a community center. The cost of
the center can be shared by all participating congregations. In a
transition neighborhood a church building being abandoned by a
congregation can often be purchased and used as a community
ministry center.

Associational program.—Many associations of churches, such as Lutheran synods, Baptist associations, and Presbyterian presbyteries, carry ministries. Some have full-time staffs. These programs depend on local congregations for funds, personnel, and sometimes for facilities. Local churches can cooperate with these agencies in ministry. In regard to juveniles, for example, a church can help pay the salary of a staff member working in juvenile rehabilitation, encourage members to open their homes to troubled young people, and supply volunteer workers for juvenile detention centers.

Project personnel.—Churches can provide personnel to other churches involved in special ministry projects. Those located in areas with great need may lack the people of skills to provide ministries. Churches with carpenters, physicians, electricians, and teachers can help. If the church in need is at a distance, the people can go on week-ends or vacations to assist. Retired persons can move to the church and live for months or even years.

Churches of Other Denominations

Churches cooperate with other denominations in evangelistic campaigns and efforts to curtail alcohol. They should also be able to cooperate in ministry. Many do. The approaches to interdenominational cooperation are similar to those between churches of the same denomination.

Clusters of churches.—Just as churches of the same denomination in an area can cooperate in ministry so can churches of several denominations. No compromises need to be made on basic doctrine. Ministry leaders from cooperating churches simply meet, plan their programs to avoid unnecessary duplication, and determine ways to share facilities and personnel.

Teams.—The team approach can also work between churches of different denominations. For example, a white Southern Baptist church and a black National Baptist church can team for ministry.

Separate community organizations.—An organization separate from but related to local churches is another means of cooperative ministry. Usually such an organization has a staff, board of directors, and legal existence all its own. Cooperating churches from different denominations supply funds, personnel, and facilities. This approach has a number of advantages. It can do what no single church can do alone. It can develop a comprehensive approach to community needs. It can reach persons who would not take part in a local church program. It can employ a staff member especially trained in ministry while many local churches cannot. A cooperative ministry may require facilities apart from those of the cooperating churches.

City-wide organization.—A city-wide interdenominational plan of ministry is similar to a neighborhood organization but is on a larger scale. It can coordinate local church programs to increase efficiency, avoid unnecessary overlap, and encourage the sharing of personnel and facilities. It can also, with a staff, develop ministries of its own. On the basis of present limited experience with city-wide organizations it appears they should coordinate rather than operate programs.

Specialized ministry.—Churches can cooperate in sponsoring specialized ministries, such as family counseling or narcotic addict rehabilitation. Such ministries use mainly professonal help, but volunteers are usually welcomed and financial support is always needed.

Denominational Ministries

Denominational agenies operate ministries such as homes for unwed mothers, adoption centers, goodwill centers, resort ministries, hospitals, homes for the aged, and homes for children. Some also have ministries to ethnic groups, migrant workers, students, and the poor. Local churches support such ministries financially. In addition, churches located nearby can provide volunteer workers, supplies, and facilities.

Interdenominational Ministries

Increasingly denominations cooperate in ministry. Several interdenominational training centers for urban ministry exist throughout the United States. These are open to all denominations. In addition, scores of interdenominational ministry are in operation. If such a ministry exists in your area, your church can consider ways to help.

Secular Private and Public Programs

Private and government-supported organizations exist in most communities to minister to human need. See Appendix A, "Community Resources," for a partial list of agencies and organizations. If a ministry is being adequately performed by one of these groups, the church may not need to duplicate it. Rather it can concentrate on ministry to unmet needs or pioneer in new approaches. Churches can cooperate with community organizations in at least three ways. A church can allow an organization to use its facilities for meetings, programs, and services. Church buildings are frequently used, for example, by Alcoholics Anonymous, Boy Scouts, literacy programs, planned parenthood associations, Headstart programs, and mental health groups. Churches can provide facilities for public health clinics and innoculation programs. The need for additional space by public schools is sometimes met by a church leasing educational space to the school system at a minimal cost.

Churches can provide staff members and volunteers for community health, education, and welfare organizations. Ministry task forces can be formed to secure competent volunteer help. By encouraging young people to enter social work professions a church can help supply staff members for community agencies.

Referring persons with need to appropriate public and private agencies is part of ministry. The church staff should keep a list of community agencies, contact persons, and telephone numbers to use in making referrals. See Appendix B for an example of such a list. Some churches have telephone referral service staffed by persons trained in counseling and community resources. People who call are given specific instructions about where to go for help. In some cases teams are dispatched to take the person where he needs to go. Churches can also cooperate by accepting referrals from a community organization. When social workers are aware that a church is prepared and willing to meet particular needs, referrals are usually made. Similarly, psychiatrists and psychologists sometimes refer persons to church counselors. It is important for a church to make known to public and private agencies what service it offers.

couraging young people to enter social work professions a church can help supply staff members for community agencies.

Referring persons with need to appropriate public and private agencies is part of ministry. The church staff should keep a list of community agencies, contact persons, and telephone numbers to use in making referrals. See Appendix B for an example of such a list. Some churches have telephone referral service staffed by persons trained in counseling and community resources. People who call are given specific instructions about where to go for help. In some cases teams are dispatched to take the person where he needs to go. Churches can also cooperate by accepting referrals from a community organization. When social workers are aware that a church is prepared and willing to meet particular needs, referrals are usually made. Similarly, psychiatrists and psychologists sometimes refer persons to church counselors. It is important for a church to make known to public and private agencies what service it offers.

II

Needs, Ministries, and Resources

The following pages list according to persons in need: (1) ministry possibilities, a list of ministries practiced or planned by churches; (2) resources, a list of local and national agencies and printed materials which supply resources for ministering to the need. The needs are in alphabetical order and are cross indexed.

Aged

(See also Retired Persons)

Ministry Possibilities

Church staff member (paid or voluntary) to coordinate programs with the aged.

Facilities for cooperative cooking and eating of meals.

Meals-on-Wheels program to provide nourishing hot meals to shut-ins.

Telephone contact to check daily on well being of the aged.

Transportation for church activities, shopping, medical care, and recreation.

Club for Bible study, recreation, trips, arts, crafts, and fellowship.

Ministry groups using services and skills of the aged. The aging can perform many ministries, such as telephone contacts, telephone census, letters to persons in institutions, teach hobby and skill classes, use professional skills in medicine, law, teaching, social work, dentistry, child care, and office work, sew, visit, operate the church library, tutor, read to the blind and handicapped, fold bulletins, mail letters, and practice intercessory prayer.

Adopt-a-Grandparent program by young adults for both institutionalized and noninstitutionalized older adults.

Tapes of worship services and religious meetings to aged.

Visits to residence (house or institution) of aged.

Activity center on ground floor of church building (or other facility) with lounge, television, games, books, and crafts for the aged.

Conferences on handling the problems of aging—medical, legal, emotional, financial, and spiritual.

Nonprofit corporation to build nursing homes and apartment buildings for the aging.

Resources

American Association of Retired People, 1225 Connecticut Ave., N.W., Washington, D. C.   20036.

National Council on the Aging, 1828 L St., N.W., Washington, D. C.   20036

National Council of Senior Citizens, 1627 K St., N.W., Washington, D. C.   20006

U. S. Department of Health, Education, and Welfare, Administration on Aging, Washington, D. C.   20201, has material available on church action.

The Church and the Aging. Board of National Missions, United Presbyterian Church, U.S.A., 475 Riverside Dr., New York, N. Y.   10027

The Church and the Older Person. Robert M. Gray and David O. Moberg. Grand Rapids: Eerdmans, 1962.

Counseling with Senior Citizens. J. Paul Brown. Philadelphia: Fortress, 1968.

How to Begin the Church Weekday Clubs Ministry from Direct Missions Dept., Baptist General Convention of Texas, Baptist Bldg., Dallas, Tex.   75201

Mission Action Resource Guide; The Aging. Woman's Missionary Union, Southern Baptist Convention, 1968.

Older Members in the Congregation. Arthur P. Rismiller. Minneapolis: Augsburg, 1964.

Alcoholic

Ministry Possibilities

AA chapter sponsored by the church.

Counseling and referral.

Crisis ministry teams on call to go and be with alcoholic in need.

Bible study and fellowship groups for alcoholics.

Fellowship groups for supportive ministry to alcoholics.

Telephone counseling and referral.

Rescue mission in area where alcoholics concentrate.

Group support meetings with families of alcoholics.

Alcohol education programs.

Homes for rehabilitating alcoholics, men and women.

Books and materials on alcohol in library and tract center.

Resources

Al-Anon Family Group Headquarters, Inc., 115 East 23rd St., New York, N.Y.   10010

General Service Board of Alcoholics Anonymous, Box 459, Grand Central Station, New York, N. Y.   10017

Alcohol In and Out of the Church. Wayne E. Oates. Nashville: Broadman, 1966.

Helping the Alcoholic and His Family. Thomas J. Shipp. Philadelphia: Fortress, 1966.

Understanding and Counseling the Alcoholic, rev. ed., Howard J. Clinebell, Jr. Nashville: Abingdon, 1968.

Apartment House Dweller

Ministry Possibilities

Rent apartment for minister to be available to residents and for worship, Bible study, group meetings, and counseling.

Chaplain for large high rise complex.

Informal groups for Bible study, discussions, therapy.

Resident professional counselor.

After school programs for children of working mothers—recreation, tutoring, study hall.

Resources

Boards of home or national missions of the larger denominations. See list of organizations in Section IV.

The Church and the Apartment House. Grace Ann Goodman. New York: United Presbyterian Church in the U.S.A.

The Church Creative. Edward Clark, ed. Nashville: Abingdon, 1967, pp. 169-77.

Faithful Rebel. Roy Blumhorst. St. Louis: Concordia, 1967.

Mission Action Group Guide: Apartment Dwellers. Brotherhood Commission, Southern Baptist Convention, 1971.

Artistic

Ministry Possibilities

Opportunities for artists to perform or exhibit their work in the church worship and educational programs.

Provide use of buildings for shows and performances.

Discussion and study groups on art forms.

Use training and skills of the artistic in ministry programs, such as coffeehouses, entertainment for the institutionalized, evangelistic rallies, recreation programs for underprivileged, and arts and crafts groups for the aging and others.

Display works in the church building.

Operate a workshop for artists as a ministry and use products in ministry, worship, decoration of church building, and other programs.

Sponsor a Festival of the Arts with artists who are members of the church and those who are not.

Offer classes in the arts taught by artists.

Program church choirs, drama groups, and bell ringing choirs.

Resources

Art teachers; local artists; art museums; theater groups; music groups.

Bereaved

(See also Widow or Widower)

Ministry Possibilities

Crisis ministry team (preferably made up of persons who have experienced similar personal bereavement) to visit and minister.

Group therapy sessions.

Counseling and referral.

Substitute on job during time of intense grief.

Care for domestic needs—food, cleaning, clothes.

Assign grief therapist to the bereaved for an extended period.

Provide helpful literature, tapes, records.

Library and tract center with material on grief.

Resources

Death and Bereavement. Austin H. Kutscher, ed. Springfield, Ill.: Charles C. Thomas, 1969.

The Dynamics of Grief. David K. Switzer. Nashville: Abingdon, 1970.

Good Grief. Granger E. Westberg. Philadelphia: Fortress Press, 1971.

Managing Grief Wisely. Stanley Cornils. Grand Rapids: Baker Book House, 1967.

Ministering to the Grief Sufferer. Charles C. Bachmann. Philadelphia: Fortress Press, 1967.

Pastoral Care of the Bereaved. Norman Autton. Naperville, Ill.: Allenson, 1967.

Ways to Wake Up Your Church. Edgar R. Trexler, ed. Philadelphia: Fortress Press, 1969, pp. 132-36.

Blind or Visually Handicapped

Ministry Possibilities

Club for the blind with Bible study, recreation, fellowship.

Medical assistance.

Provide Bibles, religious material, and other items in Braille or large print.

Make available tapes of religious services, Bible study, and other interesting topics.

Form ministry team using the blind, such as telephone counseling, referral, visitation, and check-up on the aging.

Employment assistance.

Counsel and referral.

Books and other materials on the blind in library and tract center.

Read to the blind.

Bring institutionalized to church building for programs and take programs to the institution.

Educate members on helping the blind.

Resources

Public welfare agency, physicians, schools for the blind.

American Bible Society, 1865 Broadway, New York, N.Y. 10023 Attention: Secretary for the Blind. Tapes, records, and Braille Bibles available.

American Foundation for the Blind, 15 W. 16th St., New York, N.Y. 10011. Aids and appliances for the blind. Books in Braille, larger print, and recorded.

Braille Circulating Library, Inc., 2823 W. Grace St., Richmond,

Va. Religious books in Braille and talking books.

Division for the Blind and Physically Handicapped, Library of Congress, 1291 Taylor St., N.W., Washington, D.C.   20542. Books on tape available.

Gospel Association for the Blind, Inc., 1516 122nd St., College Point, N.Y.   11356.   Publishes religious literature for the blind.

John Milton Society for the Blind. 475 Riverside Drive, New York, N.Y.   10027. Religious literature.

The Church and the Exceptional Person. Charles E. Palmer. New York: Abingdon Press, 1961, pp. 53-63, 125-27, 131.

Techniques with Tangibles: A Manual for Teaching the Blind. H. and Mary Fulker. Springfield, Ill.; Charles C. Thomas, 1968.

Childless Couple

Ministry Possibilities

Counseling concerning options: remain childless, medical correction, artificial insemination, adoption, or foster care.

Guidance to adoption agencies if adoption is their choice.

Suggest sources of children for foster care if that is their choice.

Family life conferences.

Group therapy.

Resources

Physicians, adoption agencies, homes for unwed mothers, children's homes.

Child Welfare League of America, Inc., 44 E. 23d St., New York, N. Y.   10010.

Planned Parenthood Federation of America, 810 Seventh Ave., New York, N. Y.   10019.

Counseling the Childless Couple. William T. Bassett. Philadelphia: Fortress, 1963.

Where to Go for Help. Wayne Oates and Kirk H. Neely, rev. ed. Philadelphia: Westminster, 1972, pp. 94-97, 106-113.

Deaf and Hard of Hearing

Ministry Possibilities

Special staff member for the deaf.

Groups for Bible study, fellowship, recreation.

Install hearing aids in certain pews of the church.

Medical assistance.

Classes in sign language.

Ministry groups using the deaf for services they can perform, such as writing cards and letters, filing materials, visiting deaf persons in need, counseling parents of deaf children and persons who have lost their hearing.

Employment assistance.

Books and other materials on the deaf in library and tract center.

Counsel and referral.

Group therapy.

Crisis ministry teams (preferably made up of physically handicapped persons) to aid those who have lost their hearing.

Bring institutionalized to church building for programs and take programs to the institution.

Resources

Public welfare agency, physicians, child guidance center, schools for the deaf.

Department of Language Missions, Home Mission Board, Southern Baptist Convention, 1350 Spring St., N.W., Atlanta, Ga. 30309.

Division of Educational Services, Bureau of Education for the Handicapped, Office of Education, Department of Health, Education, and Welfare, Washington, D. C. 20202. Has captioned films available.

National Association of Hearing and Speech Agencies, 919 18th St., N.W., Washington, D.C. 20006.

National Association of the Deaf, 905 Bonifant St., Silver Springs, Maryland 20910.

American Annals of the Deaf. 5 times a year. $10.00. Also an annual directory of services. Conference of American Schools for the Deaf, 5034 Wisconsin Ave., N.W., Washington, D. C. 20016.

The Church and the Exceptional Person. Charles E. Palmer. Nashville: Abingdon Press, 1961, pp. 42-51, 127, 131.

Deaf Children at Home and at School. Dion M. Dale, Springfield, Ill.: Charles C. Thomas, 1967.

Manual for Work With Deaf. Department of Language Missions, Atlanta, Ga.; Home Mission Board, SBC, 1967.

Divorcees

Ministry Possibilities

Counseling and referral.

Group therapy.

Fellowship groups for Bible study, sharing, recreation.

Day care for children.

Ministry team (perhaps of divorcees) to contact persons involved in divorce.

Family life conferences.

Books and materials in library and tract center on divorce.

Resources

Parents Without Partners, Inc., 7910 Woodmont Ave., Suite 1000, Washington, D. C.   20014.

Divorce, The Church, and Remarriage. James G. Emerson, Jr., Philadelphia: Westminster, 1961.

Explaining Divorce to Children. Earl A. Grollman, ed. Boston: Beacon, 1969.

One-Parent Family. Benjamin Schlesinger, ed. Toronto: University of Toronto Press, 1969.

Pastoral Counseling in Social Problems. Wayne E. Oates. Philadelphia: Westminster, 1966.

Raising Your Child in a Fatherless Home. Eve Jones. New York: Free Press, 1963.

Where Is Daddy? Beth Goff. Boston: Beacon, 1969.

Dying

Ministry Possibilities

Provide spiritual comfort and assurance.

Counsel on legal and financial matters.

Devotional and practical material available in library, tract center, and to visitors to take to the dying.

Grief ministry teams (preferably made up of persons who have experienced similar grief) to support the family of the dying person.

Resources

Physicians, pastors, lawyers, funeral directors.

Counseling the Dying. Margaretta K. Bowers, et al. New York: Nelson, 1964.

Explaining Death to Children. Earl A. Grollman, ed. Boston: Beacon Press, 1967.

Ministering to the Dying. Carl J. Scherzer. Philadelphia: Fortress Press, 1967.

Pastoral Care of the Dying. Norman Autton. Naperville, Ill.: Allenson, 1966.

Emotionally Disturbed

(See also Mentally Ill)

Ministry Possibilities

Full- or part-time trained counselors on the church staff.

Counseling and referral.

Group therapy.

Retreats.

Books and tracts in library, book store, tract center on dealing with emotional problems.

Provide facilities for professional counselors.

Train laymen in counseling procedure.

Recreation and fellowship opportunities.

Ministry teams (preferably made up of persons who have experienced serious emotional disorder) to help by means of visits, support, and counsel.

Resources

Mental health association, psychologists, school and family counselors, child guidance clinics.

The Church and the Exceptional Person. Charles E. Palmer. Nashville: Abingdon, 1961.

Ministering to Deeply Troubled People. Ernest E. Bruder. Philadelphia: Fortress Press, 1967.

Pastoral Care in Crucial Human Situations. Wayne Oates and Andrew D. Lester. Valley Forge: Judson Press, 1969, pp. 90-137.

Where to Go for Help. Wayne Oates and Kirk H. Neely, rev. ed. Philadelphia: Westminster, 1972. pp. 114-120.

Engaged

Ministry Possibilities

Premarital counseling.

Group sessions on preparing for marriage.

Books and other materials on marriage available in library and tract center.

Family life conferences.

Resources

Family counselors, professors of family life, psychologists, physicians.

American Association of Marriage Counselors, 149-157 Willetts Point Blvd., New York, N. Y. 10000.

Premarital Guidance. Russell L. Dicks. Philadelphia: Fortress, 1967.

Premarital Pastoral Care and Counseling. Wayne E. Oates. Nashville: Broadman, 1958.

Ethnic Group Members

(See also Non-English Speaking, Poor,
Housing Substandard)

Ministry Possibilities

Cooperate on community action improvement projects.

Tutoring.

Adult education classes.

Classes in history of the ethnic group, or how to become a citizen, or learning to speak and read English.

Conferences and discussions on the nature of prejudice and what to do about it.

Ministry teams to work for open housing.

Literacy programs.

Employment assistance in job training and placement.

Language Bible studies and worship services.

Funds for financing ethnic business projects.

Team churches—white and ethnic church cooperate in programs and ministry, such as youth retreats, deacon retreats, exchange programs of preachers, Bible study teachers, and choirs.

Scholarships for college students.

Day care and camping program.

Books and materials in library about and *by* members of ethnic groups.

Friendship program to acquaint persons of different ethnic groups with one another.

Resources

Congregational Guide for Human Relations. Commission on Research and Social Action, The American Lutheran Church, 422 S. 5th St., Minneapolis, Minn. 55415.

Mission Action Group Guide: Language Groups. Woman's Missionary Union, Southern Baptist Convention, 1967.

Mission Action Group Guide: Negroes. Brotherhood Commission, Southern Baptist Convention, 1969.

Expectant Mothers

Ministry Possibilities

Prenatal medical care.

Classes on baby care and nutrition.

Family life conferences.

Books and other materials in library and tract center on prenatal and baby care.

Medical clinics in poor areas.

Resources

Physicians; nurses; psychologists.

Advice to the Expectant Mother, 13th ed. Francis J. Browne, John C. Brown, and C. M. John. Baltimore: Williams and Wilkins, 1967.

How to Begin the Church Community Clinic Program. Direct Missions Dept., Baptist General Convention of Texas, Baptist Bldg., Dallas, Tex. 75201.

Pregnancy and You, rev. ed. Aline B. Auerback and Helene S. Arnstein. New York: Child Study Association, 1971.

Preparing for Childbirth: A Manual for Expectant Parents. Frederick W. Goodrich. Englewood Cliffs, N. J.: Prentice-Hall, 1966.

Gangs

(See also Juvenile Offender, Youth)

Ministry Possibilities

Church staff member to walk streets, meet gang members, gain confidence.

Legal aid.

Center for meetings and activities.

Discussions on social problems and what to do about them.

Act as mediator and reconciler between rival gangs.

Coffeehouse or teen club, place for youth to go for recreation and entertainment off the streets.

Conferences and information on drugs.

Resources

Juvenile court; juvenile section of the police department; public school counselors; adolescent psychologists.

Gang Delinquency and Delinquent Subcultures. James F. Short, Jr., ed. New York: Harper and Row, 1968.

Juvenile Gangs in Context. Malcolm W. Klein and Barbara G. Myerhoff, eds. Englewood Cliffs, N. J.: Prentice-Hall, 1967.

Street Gang Work: Theory and Practice. Irving Spergel. Garden City, New York: Doubleday, 1966.

Gifted Child

Ministry Possibilities

Special classes in Bible study.

Opportunities for challenging projects and experiences.

Books and materials in library for advanced reading and study.

Counsel and referral.

Resources

Public school counselors; child guidance center; child psychologists.

National Association for Gifted Children, 8080 Springfield Drive, Cincinnati, Ohio   45236.

The Church and the Exceptional Person. Charles E. Palmer. Nashville: Abingdon, 1961, pp. 33-37.

The Church: The Gifted and Retarded Child. Charles F. Kemp. St. Louis: Bethany Press, 1958.

Meaningful Religious Experience for the Bright or Gifted Child. Herbert B. Neff. New York: Association Press, 1968.

Homeless

(See also Poor, Runaway Youth, Housing Substandard)

Ministry Possibilities

Hostels for emergency housing.

Support rescue missions in transient areas.

Nonprofit corporation to build housing for low income families.

Ministry group to work *with* persons in need of housing to build houses.

Host families for temporary shelter.

Portion of church facilities equipped for emergency housing.

Resources

Public welfare agencies; Salvation Army; rescue mission.

Homosexual

Ministry Possibilities

Counseling and referral.

Group therapy sessions.

Study group to explore causes of and proper Christian responses to homosexuality.

Books and materials in library and tract center on homosexual.

Sex education program in the church.

Family life conferences.

Resources

Family counselors; psychiatrists; psychologists.

Few resources are available on church response to the homosexual. The following organizations have done more than anyone else although their approach is not approved by all churchmen:

American Association of Marriage Counselors, 149-157 Willetts Point Blvd., New York, N. Y.   10000.

Anomaly, 115 Southampton St., c/o Rescue, Inc., Boston, Mass.   02118.

The Council on Religion and the Homosexual, Inc., 330 Ellis St., San Francisco, Cal.   94102.

Glide Urban Center, 330 Ellis St., San Francisco, Cal. 94102.

Sex Information and Education Council of the U. S., 1885 Broadway, New York, N. Y.   10023.

Is Gay Good? W. Dwight Oberholtzer, ed. Philadelphia: Westminster Press, 1971.

Toward a Christian Understanding of the Homosexual. H. Kimball Jones. New York: Association Press, 1966.

Where to Go for Help. Wayne Oates and Kirk H. Neely, rev. enl. ed. Philadelphia: Westminster Press, 1972, pp. 81-84.

Hospitalized

(See also Institutionalized, Sick)

Ministry Possibilities

Brief, helpful visits, calls, and notes in keeping with best interests of the one sick.

Blood donation.

Substitute on the job for person hospitalized.

Care for domestic responsibilities—food, cleaning, washing.

Financial assistance.

Transportation for family.

Volunteer hospital duty.

Sit with person in hospital.

Provide portable television sets, reading material, and games.

Utilize the hospitalized in ministry activity when they are able—addressing envelopes, preparing party decorations, writing letters to persons in need, telephoning shut-ins.

Resources

Physicians; nurses; professors of pastoral care and counseling.

And You Visited Me: A Guide for Lay Visitors to the Sick. Carl J. Scherzer. Philadelphia: Fortress Press, 1966.

The Church and the Exceptional Person. Charles E. Palmer. Nashville: Abingdon Press, 1961.

Mission Action Group Guide: The Sick. Woman's Missionary Union, Southern Baptist Convention, 1967.

Pastor's Pocket Manual for Hospital and Sick Room. Edmond H. Babbitt. Nashville: Abingdon, 1949.

Housing Substandard

Ministry Possibilities

Credit union for loans.

Ministry group to *work with* persons in substandard housing in improving their facilities.

Nonprofit corporation to purchase substandard housing, improve it, and sell or rent to low income families.

Ministry group to work with renters in gaining improvements from landlords, especially in getting property to meet housing codes without unjustly raising rent.

Legal aid.

Housing service to help people locate suitable, low-cost housing.

Resources

Real estate agents; government housing personnel; community fair housing groups; human relations council on housing.

Office of Church and Housing, Board of National Missions, The United Presbyterian Church in the U.S.A., 475 Riverside Drive, New York, N. Y. 10027.

National Urban Coalition, 2100 M Street, N.W., Washington, D. C. 2037.

Build Brother Build. Leon H. Sullivan. Philadelphia: Macrae Smith, 1969.

Journey Inward, Journey Outward. Elizabeth O'Connor. New York: Harper and Row, 1968, pp. 37-51.

Mission Action Group Guide: Economically Disadvantaged. Woman's Missionary Union, Southern Baptist Convention, 1967.

Ways to Wake Up Your Church. Edgar R. Trexler. Philadelphia: Fortress Press, 1969, pp. 90-96.

Hungry

(See also Poor)

Ministry Possibilities

Emergency food centers.

Cooking and nutrition classes on use of government surplus food.

Cooperative farms and stores.

Hot breakfast programs for children.

Serve meals in needy areas.

Arrangement with restaurants to serve meal and charge church.

Meals-on-Wheels program to take hot lunches to undernourished people.

Resources

Public welfare departments; Salvation Army; rescue missions.

Department of Church and Economic Life, National Council of Churches, 475 Riverside Drive, New York, N. Y. 10027.

Office of Economic Opportunity, Washington, D. C. 20506.

How Churches Fight Poverty: Sixty Successful Local Projects. Elma L. Greenwood. New York: Friendship, 1967.

Hunger, U.S.A. Citizens' Board of Inquiry into Hunger and Malnutrition in the United States. Boston: Beacon, 1968.

Mission Action Group Guide: Economically Disadvantaged.
Woman's Missionary Union, Southern Baptist Convention, 1967.
Pastoral Care with the Poor. Charles F. Kemp. Nashville: Abingdon, 1972.

Institutionalized or Homebound

(See also Blind, Deaf, Mentally Ill, Mentally Retarded, Orthopedically Handicapped, Prisoners, and Sick)

Ministry Possibilities

Provide chaplain for the institution.
Bring the institutionalized to church buildings when possible for programs of Bible study, worship, fellowship, and recreation.
Take programs of Bible study, worship, fellowship, recreation, and entertainment to institution.
Personal visits with the institutionalized.
Letters, reading material, gifts to the institutionalized when permissible.
Develop a traveling entertainment group from the church to visit institutions.
Determine needs and supply them, such as reading material, barbers, grooming, recreation program, schooling.
Provide volunteers for help.

Resources

Institutional chaplains; physicians; institutional administrators.
The Church and the Exceptional Person. Charles E. Palmer. Nashville: Abingdon, 1961, pp. 83-85, 139-48.
Mission Action Group Guide: Prisoner Rehabilitation. Brotherhood Commission, Southern Baptist Convention, 1968.
Mission Action Group Guide: The Sick. Woman's Missionary Union, Southern Baptist Convention, 1967.

Internationals

(See also Non-English Speaking)

Ministry Possibilities

Program of Bible study, fellowship, trips, and discussions.
Host families to provide a place to stay during holidays, special meals, trips, and a place to visit.
Tutoring in speaking and reading English.

Conferences on laws, customs, and religious life of the United States.

Citizenship classes for those desiring citizenship.

Friendship House—a meeting place for internationals with recreation, books, television, and the presence of interested Christians.

Groups for wives of internationals to provide companionship, child care assistance, and other help.

Resources

Mission Action Group Guide: Internationals. Woman's Missionary Union, Southern Baptist Convention, 1967.

Juvenile Offender

(See also Gangs, Youth)

Ministry Possibilities

Counseling and referral.

Supply stable, Christian foster homes.

Visitation and support ministry to the institutionalized.

Provide legal assistance and appear in court with the juvenile.

Employment aid.

Tutoring service for school dropouts and slow learners.

Aggressive, balanced youth program—service projects, camps, retreats, choir, Bible study, discussion groups, athletics, recreation, vocational guidance, counseling, parent-teen dialogues.

Ministry with gangs.

Family life conferences.

Ministry teams (made up of trained, skilled, compassionate persons) available to help juveniles.

Resources

Juvenile court; denominational juvenile workers; lawyers; family counselors; psychologists.

Children's Bureau, U.S. Department of Health, Education, and Welfare, Washington, D. C.   20201.

National Council on Crime and Delinquency, 44 E. 23rd Street, New York, N. Y.   10010.

Action Programs for Delinquency Prevention. William E. Amos. Springfield, Ill.: C. C. Thomas, 1965.

Juvenile Rehabilitation. William Crews. Department of Christian

Social Ministries, Home Mission Board, Southern Baptist
Convention.

Mission Action Group Guide: Juvenile Rehabilitation. Woman's
Missionary Union, Southern Baptist Convention, 1967.

Prevention of Delinquency: Problems and Programs. John R.
Statton and Robert M. Terry, comp. New York: Macmillan, 1968.

Lonely

(See also Aged, Bereaved, Single Adults,
Widows, and Widowers)

Ministry Possibilities

Visit in their homes.

Clubs for Bible study, fellowship, recreation, and travel.

Utilize the lonely in ministry programs in which they talk with
people, such as telephone counseling or visitation of newcomers.

Provide transportation and escort to functions in which they
can participate.

Lounge or coffeehouse for conversation center.

Fellowship groups for the recently bereaved.

Telephone ministry to make frequent contact with the lonely.

Ministry team trained to locate or notice a lonely person, relate
to them, and guide them into a group of their interest.

Resources

Escape from Loneliness. Paul Tournier. Philadelphia: Westminster Press, 1962.

Farewell to the Lonely Crowd. John W. Drakeford. Waco,
Texas: Word, 1968.

Ways to Wake Up Your Church. Edgar Trexler, ed. Philadelphia: Fortress, 1969, pp. 132-36.

Marriage Conflict

Ministry Possibilities

Counseling and referral.

Crisis team (preferably of persons who have themselves sur-
vived serious marital conflict) to call on, talk with, and help
the couple.

Books and pamphlets in library and tract rack on marriage.

Family life conferences and education program.
Church staff counselor for marriage and family.

Resources

Family service organization; family counselors; psychologists; psychiatrists.

Office of the American Association of Pastoral Counselors, 31 W. 10th Street, New York, N. Y. 10011. Can supply list of agencies and counselors.

The Intimate Marriage. Charlotte H. and Howard J. Clinebell, Jr. New York: Harper and Row, 1970.

Marital Counseling. R. Lofton Hudson. Philadelphia: Fortress, 1966.

Marriage for Moderns. Henry A. Bowman. Sixth ed. New York: McGraw-Hill, 1970.

Solving Problems in Marriage: Guidelines for Christian Couples. Robert K. Bower. Grand Rapids, Michigan. Wm. B. Eerdmans, 1971.

Where to Go for Help. Wayne E. Oates and Kirk H. Neely, rev. ed. Philadelphia: Westminster Press, 1972, pp. 73-77.

Mentally Ill

Ministry Possibilities

Teams (preferably made up of persons who have experienced mental illness personally or in their family) to minister to mentally ill person and his family.

Counseling and referral.

Group sessions for families of the mentally ill.

Financial support for adequate treatment.

Education programs on mental illness.

Visitation when helpful to the institutionalized.

Employment service for person recovering from mental illness.

Utilize the mentally ill in programs of ministry to the degree they are capable, such as addressing letters, creating pieces of art for worship centers, making gifts for shut-ins, sewing for neglected children.

Stay with mentally ill person so family can be out.

Provide information and materials to families on the nature of mental illness and the care and treatment of the mentally ill.

Books and materials in library and tract center on mental illness.

Resources

Psychiatrists; psychologists; mental health association; family service organization.

National Association for Mental Health, 1800 North Kent Street, Rosslyn, Virginia   22209.

Academy of Religion and Mental Health, 16 East 34th Street, New York, N. Y.   10016.

The Christian Encounters Mental Illness. Harold Haas. St. Louis: Concordia, 1966.

Mental Illness: A Guide for the Family. Edith M. Stern. Fifth ed. New York: Harper and Row, 1968.

Ministering to Deeply Troubled People. Ernest E. Bruder. Philadelphia: Fortess, 1967.

When Religion Gets Sick. Wayne E. Oates. Philadelphia: Westminster Press, 1970.

Mentally Retarded

Ministry Possibilities

Sunday classes for retarded during Bible study and worship services.

Weekday program in church facilities.

Crisis teams (preferably made up of parents with mentally retarded children) to visit and minister to parents who have learned their child is retarded.

Conferences and group therapy for parents.

Medical assistance.

Camps, recreation, trips, and programs for the retarded.

Special facilities for weekday program for the retarded.

Employment service for the employable retarded.

Train workers for the retarded.

Visitation, recreation, and chapel programs for the institutionalized.

Volunteer aids in institutions.

Stay with the retarded to enable family to be out.

Christian education program within home of the retarded.

Provide materials and information on helping and caring for the retarded.

Utilize the retarded in ministry functions to the degree they are able, such as preparing and serving meals, making posters, repair work on houses, addressing envelopes.

Resources

Local mental health association; public welfare agencies; institutions for the retarded; physicians; special education public school teachers.

American Association on Mental Deficiency, 5201 Connecticut Avenue, N.W., Washington, D. C. 20015.

Commission on Mental Retardation, The Lutheran Church— Missouri Synod, 210 N. Broadway, St. Louis, Mo. 63102.

National Association for Mental Health, 1800 N. Kent Street, Rosslyn, Virginia 22209.

National Association for Retarded Children, 2709 Ave. E, East, Arlington, Texas 76112.

President's Committee on Mental Retardation, 7th and D Streets, S.W., Washington, D. C. 20201.

Christian Education for Retarded Persons. LaDonna Bogardus. Rev. ed. Nashville: Abingdon Press, 1969.

Helping the Retarded to Know God. Hans R. Hahn and Werner R. Raasch. St. Louis: Concordia, 1969.

How You Can Help Your Retarded Child. Edward L. French and J. Clifford Scott. Rev. ed. Philadelphia: Lippincott, 1967.

Mental Retardation: A Programmed Manual for Volunteer Workers. Alden S. Gilmore and Thomas A. Rich. Springfield, Ill.: C. C. Thomas, 1967.

Pastoral Care in Crucial Human Situations. Wayne E. Oates and Andrew D. Lester. Valley Forge, Pa.: Judson Press, 1969.

Some Approaches to Teaching Autistic Children. P. T. Weston, ed. Elmsford, N. Y.: Pergamon, 1966.

Successful Ministry to the Retarded. Elmer L. Towns and Roberta L. Graff. Chicago: Moody Press, 1972.

Where to Go for Help. Rev. enl. ed. Wayne E. Oates and Kirk H. Neely. Philadelphia: Westminster Press, 1972, pp. 121-127.

Migrant Workers

Ministry Possibilities

Child care centers providing recreation, stories, crafts, movies.
Worship and Bible study centers in mobile units.
Medical and dental clinics in mobile units.
Tutoring programs.

Study-action groups for increased wages and improved working and living conditions.

School for children.

Recreation and entertainment programs.

Resources

Time Together—Migrant Ministry Resource Book. National Council of Churches of Christ in the U.S.A., 475 Riverside Drive, New York, N. Y.   10027.

Military Personnel

Ministry Possibilities

Conferences and materials on life in the military as a Christian.

Letters, tapes, and devotional materials to men in service.

Send lists of missionaries in areas where the person is stationed.

Recognition and support when he comes home.

Books and materials in library and tract center on military service.

Provide vocational guidance, help with schooling, and employment assistance for returning servicemen.

Resources

Military personnel; military chaplains; denominational agencies responsible for chaplains.

General Commission on Chaplains and Armed Forces Personnel, 122 Maryland Avenue, N.E., Washington, D. C.   20002. *Ministry to the Armed Forces* is a very helpful book, available for $1.00.

American National Red Cross, 17th and D Sts., N.W., Washington, D. C.   20006.

Veterans Administration, Vermont Ave., N.W., Washington, D. C.   20420.

Counseling the Serviceman and His Family. Thomas A. Harris. Philadelphia: Fortress, 1966.

Mission Action Group Guide: Military. Brotherhood Commission, Southern Baptist Convention, 1968.

Narcotic Addict

Ministry Possibilities

Sponsor rehabilitation groups or invite rehabilitation groups to meet in the church building.

Provide Bible study, prayer, and fellowship groups for addicts.
Supervised housing for persons in transition from addiction.
Telephone counseling and referral.
Teams on call to go and be with person in need.
Purchase medical service for addicts.
Sponsor drug abuse center and clinic.
Employment service for persons striving to live without drugs.
Drug education program.
Counseling.

Resources

Public Health Service; physicians; drug abuse centers; narcotics division of police department.

Addicts Anonymous, Box 2000, Lexington, Ky.   41001.

American Medical Association, Mental Health and Drugs Committee, 535 N. Dearborn St., Chicago, Ill.   60610.

American Social Health Association, 1740 Broadway, New York, N. Y.   10019.

Drug Addiction Rehabilitation Enterprise, 211 Littleton Ave., Newark, N. J.   07103.

Narcotics Education, Inc., 6830 Laurel Ave., N. W., Washington, D. C.   20012.

The National Clearinghouse for Mental Health Information, 5454 Wisconsin Ave., Chevy Chase, Md.   20015.

The Drug Crisis and the Church. Henlee H. Barnette. Philadelphia: Westminster Press, 1971.

The Drug Scene. Donald B. Louria. New York: McGraw-Hill, 1968.

How Can We Teach Adolescents About Smoking, Drinking, and Drug Abuse? American Association for Health, Physical Education, and Recreation. Washington, D. C.: National Education Association, 1968.

Pot is Rot. Jean C. Vermes. New York: Association Press, 1969.

Understanding and Helping the Narcotic Addict. Tommie L. Duncan. Philadelphia: Fortress, 1968.

Where to Go for Help. Wayne E. Oates and Kirk H. Neely, rev. ed. Philadelphia: Westminster Press, 1972, pp. 153-61.

Neglected Children

Ministry Possibilities

After-school recreation.

Summer recreation and study program.

Tutoring.

Clubs for Bible study, recreation, arts, crafts, and trips.

Saturday program of entertainment, recreation, tutoring, and Bible study.

Day camp and other camping.

Families in church take them for holidays, travel, special events.

Provide small group foster care.

Promote Big Brothers of America and the Big Sister Association.

Maintain a list of persons willing to participate in foster care.

Day care with scholarships for those who could not otherwise attend.

Counseling and referral.

Resources

Local city board on parks and recreation; public welfare agency; public child welfare agencies; homes for children; public school authorities.

Child Study Association of America, 9 E. 89th St., New York, N. Y. 10028.

Children's Bureau, U. S. Dept. of Health, Education, and Welfare, Washington, D. C. 20201.

Church Community Weekday Ministries. Dept. of Christian Social Ministries, Home Mission Board of the Southern Baptist Convention.

How to Begin the Church Community Tutoring Program, How to Begin the Church Day Care Ministry, How to Begin the Church Weekday Clubs Ministry from the Direct Missions Dept., Baptist General Convention of Texas, Baptist Bldg., Dallas, Tex. 75201.

Journey Inward, Journey Outward. Elizabeth O'Connor. New York: Harper and Row, 1966, pp. 138-66.

Struggle for Integrity. Walker L. Knight. Waco, Tex.: Word, 1969, pp. 57-74.

Nicotine Addict

Ministry Possibilities

Group therapy and counseling.

Conferences on "Ways to Stop Smoking."

Education programs on the danger of nicotine.

Support groups for Bible study, prayer, and fellowship.

Retreat for smokers to deal with their problem.

Books and materials in library and tract center on smoking and health.

Resources

Physicians; local chapter of American Cancer Society and American Heart Association.

American Cancer Society, 219 E. 42nd St., New York, N. Y. 10017.

American Heart Association, 44 E. 23rd St., New York, N. Y. 10010.

National Tuberculosis and Respiratory Disease Association, 1740 Broadway, New York, N. Y. 10019.

How to Stop Smoking. Herbert Brean. New York: Pocket Books, 1970.

How Can We Teach Adolescents About Smoking, Drinking, and Drug Abuse? American Association of Health, Physical Education, and Recreation. Washington, D. C.: National Education Association, 1968.

Learning to Live Without Cigarettes. William A. Allen, et al. Garden City, N. Y.: Doubleday, 1967.

Smoking and Health. U. S. Surgeon General—Advisory Committee. New York: Van Nostrand-Reinhold, 1964.

Smoking, Health, and Behavior. Edgar F. Borgatta and Robert R. Evans, eds. Chicago: Aldine Pub. Co., 1969.

Night People

Ministry Possibilities

Telephone counseling and referral.

Protection teams in dangerous neighborhoods to escort persons to and from work or transportation.

Night care for persons, such as children, the retarded, the handicapped, and the aged, who are dependent on those who work at night.

Church building open for sanctuary and prayer at night.
Roving minister in areas where bars, prostitutes, strip shows, and night clubs are located.
All-night Christian centers for refreshment and conversation in areas of high concentration of night people.

Resources

San Francisco Council of Churches, 942 Market St., Room 502, San Francisco, California   94102.
Night Pastor of Chicago, 30 E. Oak St., Chicago, Ill.   60611.
The Church Creative. M. Edward Clark, et al., ed. New York: Abingdon Press, 1967, pp. 104-08.
The Night Pastors. Stanley G. Matthew. Hawthorn Books, Inc., 1967.

Non-English Speaking

(See also Internationals, Refugees, Ethnic Group Members)

Ministry Possibilities

Classes in the church buildings for learning to read and speak English.
Classes in becoming a citizen.
Ministry group composed of teachers and linguists to tutor and teach English at a place convenient for non-English speaking persons.
Translate worship services and Christian education sessions into appropriate languages.
Provide Bibles and other materials in appropriate languages.

Resources

Language teachers in public schools and colleges; internationals with excellent ability in English.
American Bible Society, 1865 Broadway, New York, N. Y. 10023, has Bibles and portions of Scripture available in many languages.
Mission Action Group Guide: Language Groups. Woman's Missionary Union, Southern Baptist Convention, 1967.

Nonreaders

Ministry Possibilities

Literacy training in the church building, community centers, homes, or places convenient for nonreaders.

Supply simplified religious literature and other reading material for the beginning adult reader.

Train literacy workers.

Assistance in filling out forms, documents, and other important papers.

Aid in understanding contracts, loan agreements, purchase plans, and other financial matters.

Resources

Local literacy centers; special education teachers.

For materials to use in literacy programs write:

Lit-Lit, Committee on World Literacy and Christian Literature, 475 Riverside Dr., New York, N. Y.   10027.

Laubach Literacy, Inc., Box 131, Syracuse, N. Y.   13210

"Approaches to Literacy Missions." Mildred Blankenship. Home Mission Board, Southern Baptist Convention, 1969.

Mission Action Group Guide: Nonreaders. Woman's Missionary Union, Southern Baptist Convention, 1968.

Toward World Literacy: The Each One Teach One Way. Frank C. Laubach and Robert S. Laubach, Syracuse, N. Y.: Syracuse University Press, 1960.

Orthopedically Handicapped

Ministry Possibilities

Employment service.

Counsel and referral for vocational rehabilitation.

Crisis ministry teams (preferably made up of physically handicapped persons) to aid those who have been crippled.

Medical assistance.

Ministry groups which utilize handicapped persons.

Specially equipped transportation for the orthopedically handicapped to church, shopping, recreation, and medical care.

Clubs for recreation and fellowship.

Halfway house near training center for vocational rehabilitation.

Ramps and elevators in buildings for use by the handicapped.

Collect materials for use by the Salvation Army and Goodwill Industries.

Resources

Physicians; public welfare agency; vocational rehabilitation centers; Goodwill Industries; Salvation Army.

American Public Health Association, 1015 18th St., N.W., Washington, D. C. 20036.

American Rehabilitation Counseling Association, 1607 New Hampshire Ave., N.W., Washington, D. C. 20009.

Association for the Aid of Crippled Children, 345 East 46th St., New York, N. Y. 10017.

Institute for the Crippled and Disabled, 340 East 24th St., New York, N. Y. 10010.

Muscular Dystrophy Association of America, Inc., 1790 Broadway, New York, N. Y. 10019.

National Foundation—March of Dimes, Box 200, White Plains, N. Y. 10602.

National Multiple Sclerosis Society, 257 Park Ave., South, New York, N. Y. 10010.

National Easter Seal Society for Crippled Children and Adults, 2023 W. Ogden Ave., Chicago, Ill. 60612.

United Cerebral Palsy Association, 66 E. 34th St., New York, N. Y. 10016.

The Church and the Exceptional Person. Charles E. Palmer. Nashville: Abingdon Press, 1961, pp. 63-69, 112-25, 132.

Employment for the Handicapped. Julietta K. Arthur. Nashville, Abingdon Press, 1967.

Happy Issue: My Handicap and the Church. G. Janet Tulloch. New York: Seabury Press, 1962.

Pastoral Care in Crucial Human Situations. Wayne E. Oates and Andrew D. Lester. Valley Forge, Pa.: Judson Press, 1969.

Overweight

Ministry Possibilities

Counseling.

Medical assistance.

Clubs for weight control, such as the Weight Watchers or Mind Over Platter, to provide information, group therapy, and support.

Books and materials on weight problems in the library and tract center.

Facilities and program for exercise and slimnastics groups.

Resources

Physicians; psychiatrists; psychologists; local groups of Weight Watchers.

TOPS Club (Take Off Pounds Sensibly), 4575 S. 5th St., Milwaukee, Wisconsin 53207.

W/W Twenty First Corp., (Weight Watchers), 635 Madison Ave., New York, N. Y. 10022.

There are numerous books on dieting, but it is best to consult and follow a physician's instructions.

The New Aerobics. Kenneth H. Cooper. Philadelphia: Lippincott, 1970.

The Story of Weight Watchers. Jean Nidetch. New York: New American Library, 1972.

Parents

(See also Gifted Child, Juvenile Offender, Marriage Conflict, School Dropouts, Slow Learners, Working Mother, Youth)

Ministry Possibilities

Counseling and referral.

Christian home conferences.

Library, book store, tract center with helpful books on family life. (Write the Christian Life Commission, 460 James Robertson Parkway, Nashville, Tennessee 37219, for a list of books and tracts on family.)

Fellowship and sharing meetings.

Child care for "Mother's Time Out," perhaps on a cooperative basis.

Parents' clubs for group discussions on common problems.

Professional staff counselor for family life.

Encourage parents to subscribe to parent-oriented magazines such as *Home Life* and *Parents*.

Resources

Family counselors; professors of family life; pediatricians; child psychologists. These can suggest good, up-to-date books on child development and parent-child relations.

American Parents Committee (APC), 20 E St., N.W., Washington, D. C. 20001.

Interfaith Commission on Marriage and Family, 475 Riverside Dr., Room 711, New York, N. Y. 10027.

National Congress of Parents and Teachers, 700 N. Rush St.,
Chicago, Illinois   60611.

Dare to Discipline. James Dobson. Wheaton, Ill.: Tyndale
House, 1970.

Promises to Peter. Charlie W. Shedd. Waco, Tex.: Word
Books, 1970.

Why God Gave Children Parents. David and Virginia Edens.
Nashville: Broadman Press, 1966.

Poor

(See also Housing Substandard, Hungry, Migrant Workers,
Transition Neighborhood Residents)

Ministry Possibilities

Credit union.

Day and night care of children of working parents.

Job and literacy training.

Recreation facilities and program.

Money management conferences.

Clothing, food, and household furnishings center.

Action group to renovate housing.

Nonprofit corporation to provide inexpensive housing.

Medical and dental clinics.

Cooking, sewing, and child care classes.

Transportation service for church activity, shopping, recreation,
and medical care.

Employment service.

Co-op stores for groceries and clothes.

Planned parenthood clinic.

Legal aid.

Resources

Public welfare agency; local government agency dealing with
poverty; Salvation Army.

The Churches' War on Poverty. Lyle E. Schaller. Nashville:
Abingdon Press, 1967.

*How to Begin the Church Community Clinic Program, How to
Begin the Church Day Care Program, How to Begin the
Church Weekday Clubs Ministry.* Direct Missions Dept.,
Baptist General Convention of Texas, Baptist Building,
Dallas, Texas   75201.

Mission Action Group Guide: Economically Disadvantaged.
Woman's Missionary Union, Southern Baptist Convention, 1967.

On Fighting Poverty. James L. Sundquist, ed. New York: Basic Books, 1969.

Pastoral Care with the Poor. Charles F. Kemp. Nashville: Abingdon Press, 1972.

Potential Suicide

(See also Emotionally Disturbed)

Ministry Possibilities

Counseling and referral to psychiatrist.

Telephone suicide prevention service.

Crisis ministry teams to dispatch for care of potential suicide.

Resources

American Association of Suicidology, c/o Nancy H. Allen, Dept. of Health, 2151 Berkeley Way, Berkeley, Calif. 94704.

International Association for Suicide Prevention, 2521 W. Pico Blvd., Los Angeles, California   90006.

National Save-A-Life League, 20 W. 43rd St., Suite 706, New York, N. Y.   10036.

Bibliography on Suicide and Suicide Prevention (PHS Publication No. 1969) can be obtained from the Superintendent of Documents, U. S. Government Printing Office, Washington, D. C.   20402.

God's Answer to Suicide. Warren W. Rush. New York: Vantage, 1969.

Samaritans: To Help Those Tempted to Suicide or Despair. C. Varah, ed. New York: Macmillan, 1966.

Where to Go for Help. Wayne E. Oates and Kirk H. Neely, rev. ed. Philadelphia: Westminster Press, 1972, pp. 176-98. Contains a list of suicide prevention centers in each state.

Prisoner

Ministry Possibilities

Letters, tapes, devotional material, books, gifts to prisoners.

Financial assistance to families.

Bible study, discussions, recreation, entertainment for prisoners.

Vocational training.

Provide chaplaincy program.

Counseling and ministry to families of prisoners.

Visiting prisoners.

Resources

Volunteers of America; jail or prison administrator; chaplains.

American Correctional Association, P. O. Box 10176, Woodbridge Station, Washington, D. C. 20018.

7th Step Foundation, 136 East Maple, Independence, Mo. 64050.

Mission Action Group Guide: Prisoner Rehabilitation. Brotherhood Commission, Southern Baptist Convention, 1968.

Released Offender

Ministry Possibilities

Halfway house for released offender and his family to stay during time of adjustment and finding employment.

Employment assistance.

Counseling.

Vocational training.

Emergency financial aid in form of grant or loan.

Sponsor persons on parole.

Group therapy sessions.

Utilize released offender in ministry programs such as director of halfway house or as a leader in work with prisoners.

Resources

Volunteers of America; parole and probation officers; ex-prisoners.

Ministering to Prisoners and Their Families. Henry H. Cassler and George C. Kandle. Englewood Cliffs, N. J.; Prentice-Hall, 1969.

Mission Action Group Guide: Prisoner Rehabilitation. Brotherhood Commission, Southern Baptist Convention, 1968.

Resort Area Visitors and Residents

Ministry Possibilities

Worship services and Bible study in hotels and motels.

Drive-in worship services.

Worship services and Bible study in camps, parks, and other resort areas using mobile chapels, floating chapels, outdoor facilities, or permanent buildings.

Post church address and telephone number in resort areas in case someone needs help.

Support a minister (chaplain) to resort and entertainment areas.

Outdoor worship center in conjunction with regular facilities.

Counseling center in resort area.

Trained witnesses and counselors sent among those in resort area.

Resources

The Christian Encounters the New Leisure. Rudolph F. Norden. St. Louis: Concordia, 1965.

Mission Action Group Guide: Resort Areas. Brotherhood Commission, Southern Baptist Convention, 1968.

Religion and Leisure in America. Robert Lee. Nashville: Abingdon, 1964.

Retired Persons

(See also Aged)

Ministry Possibilities

Provide activity center with games, crafts, meeting rooms.

Sponsor club for retired persons with activities such as Bible study, trips, programs, meals, parties.

Offer ministry groups to utilize skills of retired persons, such as education in preschool and nursery, financial counsel, building skills, case work, drama, secretarial, medical, and dental.

Utilize time of retired persons in programs, such as visitation, record keeping, repairs, building, baby care, medical work, telephone counsel, and referral.

Conferences on preparing for and living in retirement.

Resources

American Association of Retired Persons, 1225 Connecticut Avenue, N.W., Washington, D. C.   20036.

Mission Action Group Guide: Resort Areas. Brotherhood Commission of the Southern Baptist Convention, 1968.

Retire to Action. Julietta K. Arthur. Nashville: Abingdon, 1969.

Retirement Handbook, rev. enl. 4th ed. Henry Schmidt, ed. New York: Harper and Row, 1971.

Runaway Youth

Ministry Possibilities

Provide temporary housing and care, such as hostels, dormitories, or private homes.

Counseling and referral.

Contact and counsel with parents.

Financial assistance or transportation furnished to return home.

Foster care for those who refuse to return home.

Resources

Local juvenile officers; Salvation Army; police.

Huckleberry House for Runaways, 1 Broderick St., San Francisco, Calif. 94117.

Shaping the Church's Ministry with Youth. David M. Evans. Valley Forge, Pa.: Judson Press, 1965.

School Dropouts

Ministry Possibilities

Counseling and referral.

Programs on benefits of education.

Tutoring to prepare for reentry to school.

Family conferences.

Employment services.

Scholarships.

Special education classes in the church building, particularly for skills such as secretarial, mechanical, and bookkeeping.

Vocational guidance.

Resources

Public school personnel; special education teachers; family counselors; psychologists.

National Congress of Parents and Teachers, 700 N. Rush St., Chicago, Ill. 60611.

National Education Association, 1201 16th St., Washington, D. C. 20036.

Untapped Good: The Rehabilitation of School Dropouts. Norman M. Chansky. Springfield, Ill.: Charles C. Thomas, 1966.

Sick

(See also Hospitalized, Institutionalized)

Ministry Possibilities

Medical clinics for poor.

Care for children of sick parents.

Grocery shopping for the confined.

Transportation to medical care.

Provide domestic services—cooking, housecleaning, laundry, ironing, yard work—for the incapacitated.

Visits, calls, and letters where permissible.

Financial assistance when needed.

Crisis ministry teams (preferably made up of people who have had experiences similar to the ones of the person in need) to minister when serious, often fatal or disabling, illness strikes, such as cancer, heart disease, or muscular dystrophy.

Take their place on job where possible.

Offer courses in home nursing and the care of the sick.

Child care centers for patients located in clinic-hospital area.

Participate in volunteer programs at hospitals such as "Candy-Stripers" and "Gray Ladies."

Blood donations.

Resources

How to Begin the Church Community Clinic Program. Direct Missions Dept., Baptist General Convention of Texas, Baptist Bldg., Dallas, Tex. 75201.

Ministering to the Physically Sick. Carl J. Scherzer. Philadelphia: Fortress, 1968.

Mission Action Group Guide: The Sick. Woman's Missionary Union, Southern Baptist Convention, 1967.

Pastor's Pocket Manual for Hospital and Sickroom. Edmond H. Babbitt. Nashville: Abingdon, 1949.

Pastoral Care in Crucial Human Situations. Wayne E. Oates and Andrew D. Lester. Valley Forge: Judson Press, 1969, pp. 169-92.

Single Adults

(See also Divorce, Widow and Widower)

Ministry Possibilities

Program for Bible study, fellowship, recreation, and discussion groups.

Trips, retreats, and special events.

Offer ministry groups to utilize the special assets of many singles, such as a flexible schedule, time in the evenings, and time for meals. Examples: supper clubs for witness, evening telephone ministry, breakfasts for school children.

Conferences on special problems, such as sex, role in society, coping with society's family orientation.

Books and materials in library and tract center on single adults.

Resources

Parents Without Partners, Inc., 7910 Woodmont Ave., Suite 1000, Washington, D. C. 20014.

Urban Young Adult Action, Inc., 11th Floor, 74 Trinity Place, New York, N. Y. 10006.

The Church and the Single Person. Frances Bontroger. Scottdale, Pa.: Herald Press, 1969.

Ministry to the Young Single Adult. Elmer Townes. Grand Rapids: Baker Book House, 1971.

Slow Learners

(See also Mentally Retarded)

Ministry Possibilities

Supply teacher assistants for public schools.

In-school and after-school tutoring programs.

Conferences and group therapy for parents.

Counseling and referral.

Special church classes and retreats.

Crisis teams (preferably made up of parents who have children who are slow learners) to minister to families when they discover their child is a slow learner.

Resources

Public schools; mental health associations; special education teachers; psychologists.

Child Study Association of America, 9 E. 89th St., New York, N. Y. 10028.

How to Begin the Church Community Tutoring Program. Direct Missions Dept. Baptist General Convention of Texas, Baptist Bldg., Dallas, Tex. 75201.

Speech Handicap

Ministry Possibilities

Therapy by trained persons.

Counsel and referrals.

Group therapy with parents.

Financial assistance for therapy and medical costs.

Books and materials in library and tract center on speech handicap and therapy.

Resources

Speech therapist; public school special education teachers, child guidance center; physicians; professors of speech therapy.

Speech Communication Association, Statler Hilton Hotel, New York, N. Y.   10001.

The Church and the Exceptional Person. Charles E. Palmer. Nashville: Abingdon, 1961, pp. 69-72.

Speech and Language Delay: A Home Training Program. R. Ray Battin and C. Olaf Haug, 2nd ed. Springfield, Ill.: Charles C. Thomas, 1970.

Your Child's Experience in Speech Correction. James D. Bryden. Danville, Ill.: Interstate, 1966.

Your Child's Speech Problems. Charles Van Riper. New York: Harper and Row, 1961.

Transition Neighborhood Residents

(See also Ethnic Group Members, Housing Substandard, Poor)

Ministry Possibilities

Church to remain in neighborhood in order to provide a stabilizing factor.

Form neighborhood improvement organization.

Conferences on prejudice and discrimination and what to do about it.

Adjust church program to meet new needs of the community, such as multiple ministries.

House (or houses) in area where ministry teams live and function by helping persons in the community.

Use integrated church visiting teams in racially changing areas.

Form team relation with church in more stable area.

Resources

The Church in the Racially Changing Community. Robert L.

Wilson and James H. Davis. Nashville: Abingdon, 1966.
Confronting a Crisis. Willis Bennett. Home Mission Board, Southern Baptist Convention, 1967.
Struggle for Integrity. Walker Knight. Waco, Texas: Word, 1969.

Unemployed

Ministry Possibilities

Furnish employment service or referral to employment agency.
Vocational training and counseling using church facilities and personnel from church and community.
Provide capital for persons with ability to operate their own business.
Form nonprofit corporations to do needed work in cities (renovation of houses and apartments, building and operating parks, constructing new dwelling units) and hire the unemployed.
Supply with emergency needs of food, clothing, and shelter.
Advise on government benefits for the unemployed.

Resources

Public welfare agency; public and private employment agencies; Job Corps.
American Federation of Labor and Congress of Industrial Organizations (AFL-CIO), 815 16th St., N.W., Washington, D. C. 20006.
International Union, United Automobile, Aerospace and Agricultural Implement Workers of America (UAW), 8000 E. Jefferson, Detroit, Mich. 48214.
Build Brother Build. Leon H. Sullivan. Philadelphia: Macrae Smith, 1969.
Mission Action Group Guide: Economically Disadvantaged. Woman's Missionary Union, Southern Baptist Convention, 1967.
Pastoral Care with the Poor. Charles F. Kemp. Nashville: Abingdon, 1972.
Strategies Against Poverty. Frank Riessman and Hermine I. Popper, eds. New York: Harper and Row, 1969.

Unwed Parents

Ministry Possibilities

Counseling and referral.

Guidance to adequate home for unwed mothers.

Crisis team (preferably made up of parents of young people who have become pregnant out of marriage) to minister to youth and their parents.

Provision for continuing education during pregnancy if the girl is not allowed to continue in school.

Sex education classes.

Clinic or financial aid to insure adequate prenatal care.

Books and materials in library and tract center on unwed parents and adoption.

Resources

State and local departments of public health and child welfare agencies can provide a list of maternity homes; family counselors; physicians.

Florence Crittenton Association of America, Inc., 608 S. Dearborn, Chicago, Ill. 60605.

National Council on Illegitimacy, 44 E. 23rd St., New York, N. Y. 10010.

Abortion: The Agonizing Decision. David R. Mace. Nashville: Abingdon, 1972.

Counseling the Unwed Mother. Helen E. Terkelsen. Philadelphia: Fortress, 1967.

I'm Going to Have a Baby and I'm Not Married. Helen E. Terkelsen. Philadelphia: Fortress, 1968.

Where to Go for Help. Wayne E. Oates and Kirk H. Neely, rev. ed. Philadelphia: Westminster Press, 1972, pp. 98-105.

Widow and Widower

(See also Bereaved, Lonely)

Ministry Possibilities

Crisis team (preferably made up of persons who are widows or widowers) to minister to persons who have lost their mate.

Counseling and referral.

Child care service.

Group therapy sessions on coping with grief and loneliness.

Books and materials in library and tract center on grief, widowhood, and loneliness.

Fellowship groups of parents without partners.

Resources

Parents Without Partners, Inc. 7910 Woodmont Ave., Suite 1000, Washington, D. C. 20014.

Theos Foundation, 11609 Frankstown Rd., Pittsburgh, Pa. 15235.

Widows Consultation Center, 136 S. 57th St., New York, N. Y. 10022.

One-Parent Family. Benjamin Schlesinger, ed. Toronto: University of Toronto, 1969.

Raising Your Child in a Fatherless Home. Eve Jones. New York: Free Press, 1963.

Ways to Wake Up Your Church. Edgar R. Trexler, ed. Philadelphia: Fortress, 1969, pp. 132-36.

Working Mother

Ministry Possibilities

Child care, day and night.

Family life conferences.

Cooperative baby sitting for shopping and other needs.

Group fellowship for discussing common problems.

Resources

Child Care and Working Mothers. Florence A. Ruderman. Child Welfare League of America, 1968.

How to Begin the Church Day Care Program. Direct Missions Dept., Baptist General Convention of Texas, Baptist Bldg., Dallas, Tex. 75201.

Women at Work: Every Woman's Guide to Successful Employment. William L. O'Neill. New York: Quadrangle, 1972.

Youth

(See also Neglected Children, Runaway Youth)

Ministry Possibilities

Youth center for meetings, Bible study, prayer groups, hobbies, recreation, fellowships.

Counseling and referral for special problems.

Camps, retreats, drama, choirs, athletic programs.

Ministry projects utilizing youth, such as tutoring, day care, summer recreation programs, Vacation Bible Schools, house renovation, visits to the institutionalized and confined, perhaps a Christian Service Corps.

Coffeehouse.

Youth hostel for transient youth or youth newly arrived in city.

Draft counseling and preparation for the military.

Teen employment service.

College preparation conferences.

Halfway house for youth coming off drugs.

Vocational guidance.

Library well stocked with materials for youth.

Resources

The Church and the New Generation. Charles E. Mowry. Nashville: Abingdon, 1969.

The Church's Ministry to Youth in Trouble. David S. Schuller. St. Louis: Concordia, 1959.

Guidebook for Developing the Church Youth Program. Janet Burton. Grand Rapids: Baker Book House, 1968.

Helping Youth in Conflict. Francis I. Frellick. Philadelphia: Fortress, 1968.

It's Tough Growing Up. C. W. Brister. Nashville: Broadman Press, 1971.

III

Examples of Ministry

This section contains examples of ministries by churches. Each ministry is listed in alphabetical order and is briefly described. Some have suggested resources. The ministries are selected from hundreds in operation or being planned.

Adopt-a-Building Program

The overwhelming vastness of the numbers of people, needs, and territory make ministering in the city difficult. In order to break the challenge down into manageable units, a church can major on one building or high-rise complex. This can be done by a suburban church interested in ministering to the inner city, by an inner-city church trying to minister in its own neighborhood, or by a combination of the two. Generally the approach is for the church or churches involved to survey the apartments, determine the needs, and map out a strategy for meeting those needs. In some instances needs will consist of renovation, repairs, working to see that the landlord meets the building code. It may be necessary to form the renters into some sort of a cooperative unit for action. In other complexes the needs may be more for counseling, spiritual guidance, and referral services. Some buildings may need provision for care of children and the aged, special programs for the retarded, or tutoring those rejected from the public schools. This is similar to the block partner program except that it majors on residence units.

Adult Education Classes

With increased leisure adults have time to expand their education. Many are eager to learn and to discover new interests. A church can minister to adults seeking education and training. Classes can range from personal improvement classes, such as classes in health, grooming, homemaking, and mental health, to classes in academic areas such as history, international affairs, and English literature. Some

90

may want to learn a language other than English to prepare for ministry to language groups. Others may want to study to prepare for ministry to the handicapped, aged, delinquent, narcotic addict, mentally ill, or retarded child. Some may want classes in religion such as church history, Christian ethics, Old Testament, New Testament, and theology. Such classes ought to be offered at a variety of times and in numerous places. A curriculum can be developed and published so that persons know when and where particular classes are offered.

Most denominations have agencies responsible for educational materials and programs. These can supply some units for adult education. Public schools, nearby colleges and universities, and seminaries can provide information for curriculum and in some cases teachers. Public schools, shopping centers and banks with conferences rooms, and other places with facilities usable for such adult education classes should be contacted about utilizing these facilities.

After-School Activities

Churches are often situated in neighborhoods where children have little or no supervision after school. This can be true in both high income as well as low income areas. By providing meaningful, exciting after-school activity for children, churches render a significant ministry as well as gain entree into homes. Such activity will vary greatly according to age groups. For younger children games, outside recreation, and inside crafts and activities may suffice. For older children organized play, competitive sports, crafts, discussions of interesting subjects, or films are necessary ingredients. Organized clubs, study halls, and tutoring sessions often can be a part of after-school activity. Although adults are needed to supervise the activities, older youth are able to lead the younger children in many programs. For further information see *How to Begin the Church Community Tutoring Program* and *How to Begin the Church Weekday Club Ministry* from the Direct Missions Department, Baptist General Convention of Texas, Baptist Building, Dallas, Texas 75201.

Amigos

In most cities persons from different economic classes and races do not know one another. There is little opportunity for dialogue, fellowship, or even casual contact. The amigos program is designed to bridge the economic and racial gaps, establish communications with different groups, and open up areas of understanding. It requires an aggressive group of people to contact individuals and families from various racial and social groups within the city, arrange for fellowship times, and encourage private follow-up gatherings.

Art Festival

A church can deepen its members' understanding of art, relate artists to the church, and demonstrate concern for total life by sponsoring an art festival. In such a festival, artists both within and outside of the church are invited to display their work. Paintings and sculpture are exhibited in the church facilities. Musicians perform. Concerts are held. Fine movies are shown. Drama groups present plays. In addition to the display of works of art, discussions and conferences are held concerning art, the relation of art and religion, and the significant themes with which art deals. For further information see *The Church Creative* edited by Edward Clark and others, Abingdon Press, 1967, pp. 109-39, *Journey Inward, Journey Outward* by Elizabeth O'Connor, Harper and Row, 1968, pp. 62-76, and *Tomorrow's Church* by William A. Holmes, Abingdon Press, 1968, pp. 105-33.

Arts, Crafts, Hobby Classes

With increased leisure people need creative ways to occupy the added time apart from vocation. Churches can guide people in developing skills and creative ability. Classes in the arts, in crafts, and in hobbies are helpful for this purpose. The possible areas covered in such classes are almost limitless. Such classes could include the following: painting, sculpturing, music, drama, leatherwork, weaving, sewing, cooking, cake decorating, hat making, flower growing and arranging, stamp collecting, coin collecting, woodworking, creative writing, ceramics, decoupaging, knitting, rock collecting and polishing, photography, movie making, camping, hiking, and basketmaking. Such classes fulfil several needs. The teachers are helped by being able to help others. The students benefit from learning new skills and ways to express themselves. The material produced can be used as gifts, decorations for church functions, and items to stock a store in order to earn money for other ministry programs. These classes can be offered in various places—church buildings, in special facilities made available to the church or leased in hospitals and other institutions, and in homes. Teachers within the public schools, persons noted for their hobbies, artists, craftsmen, and individuals working in craft and hobby stores can be helpful resources.

Baby Sitting Co-op

The emotional health of many mothers could be improved if they had opportunity to be away from their children for periods of time during a week. For many this is difficult either because there are no qualified baby sitters available or because they cannot afford a baby sitter. The church can provide short-term child care in the church facilities. It can establish a cooperative baby sitting program. In such a program a number of mothers living near one another form a co-op. A mother receives a certain number of points, for keeping a child for a period of time. The mothers trade out baby sitting, keep a record of the points, and thus insure that no one carries a disproportionate load. At the end of the year the points are totaled. Those with extra points are paid a certain amount per point. Those with fewer points pay this bill. Often such a cooperative involves the church only in suggesting the idea and helping organize the groups.

Block Partners

Suburban churches frequently find it difficult to minister in the inner city. Several approaches are workable. Team ministries between a suburban and an inner-city church or an extension of a suburban church located in the inner city are options. Another approach is not related specifically to a church in the inner city but rather to an area. A suburban church adopts a block in the inner city as its particular project. The church anlyzes the block as to needs for education, housing, health, employment, and family services. The church then forms teams of experts in these areas to work with the residents in mapping out practical, appropriate programs. This plan has the advantage of linking the people in the suburbs who frequently have access to the power structure of the city with the persons in the inner city who have the greatest needs. It also puts together people who know what it is like in the inner city with those who have only theories about inner-city problems. It has a further advantage in that it majors on a manageable geographic area rather than on an entire region or inner-city sector.

Book Store

Some churches have found a book store to be as vital to ministry as a library. Books on ministry and specific personal needs are stocked. People can purchase their own book, mark it as they please, and refer to it again and again. Some churches have books available throughout the year. Others make them available only during special emphases. A well-stocked and operated store in a large church can earn money for expanding the book store stock, adding to the library, or funding other ministry programs.

Some churches operate book stores in buildings apart from the church facilities. Such stores stock a wide variety of books but major on those relating to personal problems, social issues, and ministry. Contact a book store for information on establishing a book sales operation.

Breakfast for Preschool Children

In many neighborhoods, particularly in the inner city, children do not get an adequate breakfast. Most of these children will receive hot lunches in school. But hot nourishing breakfasts to begin the day are rare. Churches can supply such breakfasts plus recreation, activity, Bible stories, and other creative activities. If a church is located in an area of need, the church building itself can be utilized. A church not located in such an area can cooperate with one which is. During warm weather it might be possible for a church to use mobile kitchens to feed the children in parking lot areas. Such programs should be more than soup kitchens. The children and the parents need to feel that this is a genuine ministry to the whole child. The breakfast should be simply part of an overall preschool program. If only breakfasts are served it appears too much like charity for the poor rather than a service to the children. Retired persons, women whose children are no longer at home, men and women whose work does not begin early, and high school students are all prime prospects for staffing a preschool breakfast-activity program. Be sure to check on and comply with all government regulations for food service.

Camping

Camping programs can be an effective part of ministry. Youth and children particularly can benefit. But so also can single adults, married adults, and retired persons. Family camping can provide opportunities to strengthen family relationships. Some churches have their own camping facilities. Others use denominational camps or state parks. Camping trips can be for long periods of time, a weekend, overnight, or even a day camping experience. It is particularly effective to take children from the inner city to expose them to outdoor life. Camps also afford an excellent opportunity for developing counseling relationships.

Care for Dependent Persons

Day care is usually thought of in relation to children of working mothers. But care programs are needed, both day and night, for many different people, including the mentally retarded, the severely physically handicapped, and the aged. Anyone who cannot stay by himself needs some type of care when other members of the family must work. Churches can care for persons needing constant supervision in families unable to afford such care. Church facilities can be used in many cases. Public welfare offices, the mental health association, and physicians can offer suggestions about such programs. Some will provide only custodial care, others education and entertainment. For additional information see *How to Begin the Church Day Care Program,* Direct Missions Department, Baptist Building, Dallas, Texas 75201.

Charm and Grooming Classes

Persons young and old are interested in hair styling, dress, and good grooming in general. A church can minister through charm and grooming classes to people who are concerned about their appearance. Although teen-age girls are likely to be the most responsive to such a program, many others from different age groups will also take part. The classes should be taught by persons who are themselves attractive. Beauticians, models, clothing salesmen, and actors are possible teachers for these classes. The classes should be oriented around the concept of Christian concern for all of life and the theme that a Christian should be attractive. Stress the idea that real beauty is inner, not outer. Effort ought to be made to emphasize that good grooming need not be costly. Also, persons should be alerted to the ways in which salesmen and advertisers prey upon human emotion and insecurity to sell products. The classes should build self-confidence, an acceptance of one's limitations, and an understanding of how an individual can be attractive while he may not be handsome or she may not be beautiful. Contact a local modeling school, charm school, or beauty school for suggestions on what to include in such a program.

Child Care Near Employment Centers

Child care services are especially needed near employment centers where large numbers of mothers work. Such centers provide convenient places for mothers to leave their children, visit with them at noon, and pick them up in the evening. These centers can be operated as a normal day care program. In addition, special child guidance and enrichment programs can be offered.

Child Care Near Hospital District

Churches located in hospital districts can minister to persons by providing short-term child care. Parents visiting in a hospital or going to a doctor's office may not want to take their children. Yet there may be no one with whom the children can be left. A convenient place for the children would be near the hospital or the doctor's office. Well publicized through announcements left in hospitals and doctors' offices, such a program will receive wide support. It is possible in some areas for the program to be subsidized by physicians. Using church facilities and volunteer workers the expenses can be kept low. A small fee could be charged or the service could be rendered without charge.

Child Care—Short Term

There is need in most communities for short-term child care. Mothers going on shopping trips, taking other children to meetings, participating in mission action programs, and involved in other worthwhile activities need a dependable place to leave their children. Many ministry programs could be performed by mothers if they had care for their children. Short-term child care can stimulate the other ministry programs of a church. The program can utilize the nursery and elementary facilities of a local church. It can be under the direction of a full-time paid worker with volunteer help. Or it can simply be staffed by volunteers working on a cooperative basis.

For further information see *How to Begin the Church Day Care Program,* Direct Missions Department, Baptist General Convention of Texas, Baptist Building, Dallas, Texas   75201.

Christian Bar

After work in the afternoon and at night there are few places single Christians can go to unwind. A ministry could be performed by establishing what would amount to a Christian bar—a place for people to gather in an unstructured setting with light snacks and delicious, but nonalcoholic, drinks. Made attractive enough and offering good enough fare, such a place would attract non-Christians as well as Christians. In the informal, unstructured setting there would be opportunity for discussions and Christian witness.

Christian Night Club

In many communities there is a lack of wholesome, quality entertainment. A church or group of churches could provide a place which serves excellent meals in attractive surroundings with superb entertainment. While the place might not have a distinctly Christian theme, it could feature entertainers who are notable Christians. Persons such as Roy Rogers and Dale Evans, Pat Boone, Tom Lester, and others could entertain and give a Christian testimony. Also, local persons who are outstanding Christian entertainers could be used. Hopefully such an operation would at least break even. But it might be necessary for subsidy to be made either in the form of volunteer help or cash.

Christian Restaurant

A cross between a Christian night club and a Christian coffeehouse, the Christian restaurant serves good food at reasonable prices during the day. It operates with a distinct Christian atmosphere in regard to symbols, materials available, counselors, and especially trained waiters. Workers could be available to sit and to talk with persons while they eat, engaging them in conversations relating to significant life issues. Such a place can cater to youth in a location close to a college or a high school. It provides a spot for youth to gather in an atmosphere conducive to positive development rather than destructive habits.

Citizenship Classes

Many immigrants and refugees would like to become citizens of the United States. The process is not a simple one and these people often need guidance, special education, and support. Churches can render service by offering classes which help prepare for the process of becoming a citizen. Most anyone can teach these classes. They can meet either in the church facilities or at another place convenient for those who want to enrol. For further information contact the Immigration and Naturalization Service, 119 D Street, N.E., Washington, D. C. 20536 (or the district office near you) for information and forms for naturalization. A booklet, the *DAR Manual*, is furnished each applicant.

Classes in Domestic Skills

Many churches offer classes in domestic skills, such as cooking, sewing, cleaning, and shopping. In poverty areas such classes can provide money-saving techniques and improve homelife. In middle and upper class areas such classes can not only improve homelife but also develop hobby skills. Such classes should be geared to the persons involved and their needs. A cooking class in a high income area obviously would be different from one in a poverty sector. The poor need to learn how to prepare surplus food items in appetizing ways. They need to know how to take clothes picked up in thrift stores or in free clothing centers and remake them to be fashionable and attractive. Numerous people are able to teach such classes. Home economics teachers, county home demonstration agents, skilled homemakers, and students majoring in homemaking skills make excellent teachers. Churches can provide both teachers and facilities. This calls for not only a place to meet but tools with which to work, such as sewing machines, material, stoves, and food. For further information see *The Mission Action Group Guide: Economically Disadvantaged,* Woman's Missionary Union, Southern Baptist Convention.

Clothing Center

In poverty areas adequate clothing is often a problem. Many churches have established a clothing center. Such a center collects clothing, sorts and sizes it, cleans it, and stores it for persons in need. In some situations a small charge is made for the clothing. Persons often prefer to pay something for the clothing—even a small amount —than to get it free. Other centers make the clothing available at whatever price a person can afford. The clothing center should be located near the persons in need since they often lack transportation facilities. Some churches keep a list of all persons who visit the center with their addresses. This information is used in follow-up visitation to minister to total need. The Salvation Army, Goodwill Industries, goodwill centers, and rescue missions are experienced in operating clothing centers. They can offer helpful advice. Also, if a church is not suitably located for such a project, clothing can be contributed to such groups.

Clubs

Many churches utilize clubs in their ministry program for boys, girls, mothers, senior citizens, internationals, and parents. These clubs usually provide activities such as Bible study, recreation, crafts, hobbies, and discussion groups. Special interest functions are also carried out. For example, a senior citizens club might take trips to interesting places, provide frequent fellowship meals, and establish a senior citizens lounge for games, hobbies, and crafts. A boys club might study auto mechanics, marksmanship, wrestling, or electronics. A mothers club might have sessions on sewing, cooking, and budget planning. For further information see *How to Begin the Church Weekday Club Ministry,* Direct Missions Department, Baptist General Convention of Texas, Baptist Building, Dallas, Texas   75201.

Coffeehouse

Various churches have found coffeehouses an effective way to minister. Coffeehouses come in many shapes and sizes. Some are primarily for youth while others are for adults. Some have overt religious emphases while others are more subdued in their religious approach. Some offer entertainment and programs, others simply provide a place with atmosphere to sit and talk. The success of the coffeehouse depends largely on a group of people well trained and committed to carrying the operation through in spite of setbacks and difficulties. Coffeehouses serve many purposes. They get youth off of the streets into a place of relative security. They offer an opportunity to sit and talk, to explore life's most significant questions. They provide a setting for persons to make acquaintances which can be deepened into lasting friendships and significant verbal witnessing opportunities. Several books provide helpful insights into the operation of coffeehouses. The following are very helpful: *The Coffee House Ministry* by John D. Perry, Jr; *God Squad* by Alice Miller; *Journey Inward, Journey Outward* by Elizabeth O'Conner.

Community Center

Many communities lack a place where meetings can be held, education courses offered, health clinics set up, and other functions conducted. Often a church has buildings well situated and usable for such purposes. A church can allow its buildings to be used for these community activities. In so doing they make clear that the church exists to serve. The practice also makes the church building appear to be open rather than closed to the people of the community. It also accustoms people to being in and out of the church facility. If the community lacks a community center facility and the church building is not adequate for such a facility, then the church in conjunction with others can help to establish a community center. A church can also play a vital role in programing the center, with such activities as health education, clinics, planned parenthood conferences, adult education classes, clubs, domestic skill classes, town hall sessions, and other activities.

Community Listening Teams

Important meetings of public officials often go unattended by representatives from the community. Churches can appoint listening teams to sit in on these meetings, note what takes place, and report back to the church for information and sometimes for action. If listening teams sense that something is being done which is unethical, unjust, or harmful, they should try to motivate necessary corrective action. The presence of such listening teams encourages public officials to be honest in their activity and to deal with serious community problems.

Community Study Groups

Community study groups can be sponsored by a local church to make a concentrated study on particular community issues, gather all available facts, interpret the facts, search for solutions, and develop certain proposals and alternate programs. Study groups can give their material to community or government agencies. Or they may become action groups. On issues affecting the entire church, study groups should be requested to present their report to church meetings. It is not necessary for the church to take action, but the church should be informed about the group's findings. Out of such reports may come action groups. These may not be official parts of the church, but bodies of concerned Christians interested in acting to correct problems.

Companion Church Program

Churches of different races linking together in a team ministry can improve interracial understanding. The participating churches can be from any two ethnic or language groups, such as a black and a white church, an Anglo and a Mexican church, or a black and an Oriental church. A number of programs can be carried out by churches linked in a team ministry. Often the ethnic church will be located in a transition or poverty area. A wealthier white church can better understand the problems in these areas by conferences and discussions with members from the team church. Also, the churches can work together in various ministries in the transition or poverty area, such as literacy classes, job training, counseling, and weekday programs of recreation, tutoring, and classes. The two churches can also participate in joint retreats, youth camps, leadership conferences, teacher training programs, and evangelistic outreaches. They can exchange pastors, choirs, and Sunday School teachers.

Consumer Skills Education

Many people, especially the poor, are often the victims of unscrupulous businessmen. The victims often pay more for goods and interest and are charged more for services than the more alert and educated middle and upper class shopper. Classes in consumer skills are appropriate in any neighborhood. Budgets of all families need stretching. But such classes are particularly helpful in poverty areas. In a consumer education course a lawyer can describe some of the legal pitfalls to avoid in signing contracts and purchasing goods. Many people buy on time payment plans completely unaware that the paper will be sold by the store to a finance company leaving the individual no legal recourse to the store if the goods are not as represented. A banker could present the problems of borrowing money from loan sharks and point out some possible sources of funds at lower costs of interest than most poor people pay. Home economists, advertising men, and marketing specialists could alert the consumer to certain advertising and marketing practices which victimize many. The Better Business Bureau is a helpful source of information on fraudulent and unscrupulous business practices.

Craft Center

A church can establish a craft center where persons watch craftsmen at work, take lessons, and purchase goods. It should be established in a place where there is a great deal of traffic, such as in a shopping center or on a busy downtown street. Christian craftsmen can talk with people as they work, explaining what they do, their feelings concerning life and faith, and the therapeutic value of the creative use of one's hands. Pottery, weaving, leatherwork, metalwork, woodwork, and sculpturing are some of the craft possibilities. See Elizabeth O'Connor's *Journey Inward, Journey Outward* for a description of the craft-art center of The Church of the Savior, Washington, D. C.

Credit Union

The poor are often unable to obtain loans through normal channels. Many banks and savings and loan associations will not make loans to persons in poverty. Most credit unions are operated for specific groups such as teachers, employees of certain companies, or fraternal organizations. Finance companies charging high interest rates or loan sharks are about the only sources for loans the poor have. A credit union established at a church can help deal with this problem. Church members own shares in the credit union, make deposits, earn interest, and draw out money in loans. The credit union must be founded and operated according to sound financial procedures. It makes possible the purchase of homes, automobiles, and major appliances at reasonable rates of interest by persons who otherwise would be unable to acquire them. It encourages saving and fiscal responsibility. A church can contact Christian bankers, executive and denominational offices dealing with finance, and government banking officials for information on setting up a credit union.

Counseling

Churches provide counseling services for members and others in various degrees and forms. The most common is pastoral care and counseling. Some churches have trained the leaders of the church to be effective in counseling. Others utilize the services of professional counselors within their membership. A few churches have on the church staff full-time professionally trained counselors. Some provide counseling facilities in the church. If a church is located near a counselor training center it can utilize trainees in its program. In several cities churches have developed a community counseling service. The cost is largely paid by the churches. They in turn refer persons to the service for counseling.

Drama

Drama can be an integral part of a ministry program. Drama in the form of skits, short plays, and full-length productions serves as a means of communicating the gospel, utilizing skills and training, and providing entertainment and recreation. Drama can be used as a part of therapy programs and serve as the basis for discussions of personal problems and social issues. Drama can also be a means of enlisting non-Christians in church-related activity.

Drug Prevention Center

A church-sponsored center can serve as the base for an education program on drug abuse. A speakers' bureau, films, and pamphlets can be stocked and used for community programs, public school assemblies, and church meetings. Rehabilitated drug abusers can give personal testimony about the damage of drugs and the necessity of avoiding their use. The drug center can also operate a twenty-four hour telephone counseling and referral service. This makes it possible for a person having trouble with drugs to call, talk to someone, and receive help. A team prepared to go and be with a person in trouble is another possible ingredient of the center.

Educational Ministry

The educational program of a church can relate to ministry. Bible study can be offered for special groups, such as the blind, the deaf, the mentally ill, the emotionally disturbed, and the mentally retarded. Church Training groups can be an integral part of ministry. Church Training can equip persons to help the alcoholic, unwed mother, narcotic addict, chronically unemployed, prisoner, juvenile delinquent, retarded, mentally ill, and others. Other programs can utilize the facility and materials of the regular educational program of the church. Tutoring programs, adult education, citizenship classes, and vocational training are examples. Human need and social problems are often the subject to study. Church groups can become aware of issues and how to deal with them.

Emergency Domestic Help

Persons often need emergency help when accident, death, or sudden illness strikes. Church task forces can provide transportation, child care, and domestic help. Or the church office can serve as a clearinghouse for matching persons in need with individuals willing to undertake such emergency services. Or a telephone task force can be formed to care for emergency needs. The book *As Close As the Telephone* by Alan Walker suggests ways in which a telephone service can help link persons in need with people willing to help.

Employment Opportunities

A church's ministry program can include efforts to find employment for able persons. Some churches have done this for teen-agers, particularly in the summer. Others have been involved in employment placement informally through the work of pastors and members of the church. A more formal and organized program is often needed. Such a program actively enlists potential employers to agree to hire unemployed persons recommended by the church's committee on employment. When jobs do not exist, a church can help develop new work opportunities. By participating in community improvement projects and efforts to secure new business a church contributes to employment. A church can also start programs to increase employment. Housing rehabilitation projects, for example, can use the unemployed. A church could establish a nonprofit corporation for rehabilitating old houses or building new low-cost housing. The corporation could then hire unemployed persons for the work. Hopefully the proceeds from the rent or sale of the property would capitalize further projects.

English Classes

Millions in the United States are handicapped because of lack of ability to use English. A church can teach these people to speak and to read English. Such classes can be taught in church buildings or in other convenient facilities. Classes can be taught by school language teachers, university professors, or persons proficient in two languages such as missionaries home on furlough. These classes can also include information about the history and culture of the United States. For further information see *Mission Action Group Guide: Language Groups,* Woman's Missionary Union, Southern Baptist Convention.

Family Life Program

The key to preventing and correcting many problems is the family. Troubled families tend to produce troubled people and contribute to a disordered society. By improving family life a church can render widespread ministry. A family ministry should include conferences, retreats, books and pamphlets, personal counseling, group counseling, and referral. The program should relate to all aspects of family life: all age groups in all family relationships; normal family operation and crisis times. The program should be directed toward those preparing for marriage, the newly married, young parents, parents of young children, parents of teen-agers, teen-agers, the middle aged, the retired, the elderly, and in-laws. Family physicians, lawyers, bankers, professors of family life, and persons recognized as having succeeded in family life can serve as valuable resources for family life programs and counseling.

Fellowship Groups

The ministry program of churches often includes fellowship groups to bring together persons of common interests and problems— alcoholics, rehabilitated drug abusers, widows and widowers, parents of teen-agers, parents of exceptional children, families of persons in prison, and families of persons suffering mental illness. Such groups afford excellent opportunities for group therapy. They often gather for prayer, Bible study, and sharing of problems and insights. For further information see *New Life in the Church* by Robert A. Raines, *Spiritual Renewal Through Personal Groups* by John Casteel, and *Farewell to the Lonely Crowd* by John Drakeford.

Financial Planning and Advice

Some people are always in financial hot water. This affects not only their personal attitudes but also their family, work, and spiritual life. The church can minister to these people by providing financial counsel and guidance. For the poor this could mean budget planning, consumer education, and classes in domestic skills. A credit union which encourages consistent saving might also be helpful. For middle and upper income families special conferences on finance and budget planning are often useful. Some churches have crisis teams made up of professional financiers who go over a person's finances and offer suggestions. Many people need pastoral counseling on how to cope with materialism.

Food Center

In poverty areas many persons are often hungry. Although government food stamp programs and surplus food items are available, there is still frequently need for good food. A church can help supply food. Several approaches are possible. A food center can be stocked by contributions of church members. A more efficient way is for members to contribute money for purchasing food. If a church can buy food through a wholesale distributor, it can purchase more food for the same amount of money than individuals can. In addition it can stock the proper variety. Another approach is for a church to have an agreement with grocery stores in poverty areas to sell groceries to persons on credit authorized by the church. This plan has merit in making a man appear to be more of a provider in the eyes of his household than when a church group brings in groceries. It has some disadvantages too. Those buying the groceries may not be skilled consumers. There are two other possibilities, both of which are more controversial than the preceding. One is for the church to operate a grocery store using volunteer help and purchasing groceries at wholesale prices. Operating in low-rent quarters with volunteer help, the price of groceries can be kept somewhat lower than those obtained in regular stores. This pits the church against private business, however. Another possibility is for the church to lead the way in establishing a grocery cooperative. In such an arrangement the people own the store, receive rebates on purchases according to the amount they buy, and contribute volunteer labor in order to lower costs. It is even possible for such a co-op to be related to a church-owned farming operation supplying many of the goods sold in the store. A farm could also serve as a rehabilitation center for alcoholics and narcotics and a halfway house for released offenders.

In such an operation the church is serving a number of persons through the interrelated projects of farming, processing, and marketing.

Form-Fill-out Assistance

In an age of bureaucracy there are many forms to fill out—for medical assistance, social security, insurance, and many others. The ill-educated, the aged, the retarded, and the mentally ill have difficulty with these forms. A church can make available persons who are skilled in understanding these forms and who can help people fill them out. Those working in such a ministry should also be trained to know what benefits are available for certain classes of people. Then they can encourage people to apply for full benefits under existing programs.

Foster Home Care

In almost every community, especially large cities, there is need for foster home care for dependent and neglected children. Many children for various legal reasons are not eligible for adoption. The care for them in institutions, even at best, would be inferior to care in a good, Christian foster home. Churches can minister by encouraging members to offer their homes for foster care. A foster care committee can secure the names of people who agree to serve as foster parents and provide these names to the court. Contact the child welfare unit in your county or write the Department of Public Welfare in your state for information on foster home care.

Fund for Justice

On occasions a church may need money to help in special causes for justice. For example, a group of tenants may need help in bringing pressure to bear on a landlord to abide by housing codes to make housing safe and decent. An individual who has been arrested and excessive bail set may need money for the bail. Members of ethnic groups endeavoring to go into business may need the capital to get started. A church can set aside money for such projects, appoint a committee to oversee the administration of the fund, and review the need for the amount annually.

Furniture and Household Goods

The poor and families hit by fire, storm, or flood often need help getting adequate furniture and other household goods. Churches can maintain a storeroom for such items. The materials can be contributed by church members and others in the community. Persons skilled in the repair of furniture and appliances can renovate them. Goods can be supplied to those in need free or at a small cost. The names and addresses of those who utilize the storeroom should be kept on file for follow-up visits and counsel.

Grief Therapy

There is usually considerable support and help for the bereaved immediately following the loss of a loved one. But then life resumes its normal pace for most and the grief stricken are left to struggle alone. The church can perform a ministry by developing group therapy for the bereaved and by training individuals to work as grief therapists. An individual grief therapist can be assigned to the bereaved for a year following the death of a loved one. The assignment is to lend support, help make necessary adjustments, and be a concerned listener.

Halfway Houses

Persons suffering from certain problems, particularly those who have been institutionalized, may need a halfway house from which to enter society again. Churches can sponsor a halfway house. Persons in need of halfway houses include alcoholics, rehabilitating narcotic addicts, prisoners, delinquents who have been institutionalized, and persons recently handicapped. Halfway houses provide a place where a person can feel secure, receive counsel, and have support from people of similar background.

Headliners

Headliners is the name for a program in which people scan newspapers and listen to news broadcasts in search of persons in need. Headliners is more of a resource group to other ministry teams rather than a direct ministry operation in itself. When they locate someone in need, the headliners contact the appropriate ministry team which then goes into action. For example, if a news story indicates that a family has been severely injured in an automobile accident, the headliners will notify the pastor or the appropriate ministry team to visit the family and find what service can be rendered. If the headliners discover a family has lost its house through fire, a ministry team can go into operation to find temporary housing, furnish clothes, and help in other ways. The headliners also can operate as a condolence, congratulation, and support ministry. When they locate someone who has suffered grief, they can drop a note of sympathy, express concern, and offer help. When they find someone has received an honor, they can send congratulations. When they realize someone is in need of encouragement and support, they can write an appropriate letter. Public officials in decision-making time, national leaders in time of crisis, and denominational leaders in the midst of controversy are examples of persons who can benefit from a word of encouragement and indication of prayer support.

Health Education

Health education is needed by all, especially those in poverty areas. The public health department and the public schools carry on health education programs. But many persons do not come into contact with these programs. Churches can provide health education through their regular curriculum, special conferences, clinics, and distribution of pamphlets and materials. Subjects to include are diet and health, personal hygiene, birth control, venereal disease, and nursing of the sick. Public health offices can supply materials and information on a health education program. In some cases they may supply personnel to help. Or the church can provide the facilities and health department people can teach the classes.

Home Handyman Service

The physically handicapped and women living alone often have difficulty with home repairs. Such repairs are frequently costly and these people usually live on limited budgets. A church can minister by forming teams of persons who can do minor repairs, carpentry, electrical work, and plumbing. These teams can operate one of two ways. They can make regular rounds of persons who are unable to do their own repair work. Or they can stand by and respond to a call. A combination of the two is perhaps the best approach. In both cases publicity about such services should be distributed. Retired persons and skilled workmen who volunteer an evening or a weekend are resources for such a program.

Homes for Runaway Youth

Young people who run away from home frequently want to return. Sometimes this is difficult. They either fear their parents' reaction or they have wandered so far away they lack adequate finances to return. Others don't want to return home but they desire to escape a way of life which they have found harmful, such as living in a drug-oriented commune. A church can minister by establishing a home for runaway youth. By advertising in local papers, especially youth papers, leaflets, and posters such a center can become widely known. Youth are invited to participate in the program with the assurance that they will neither be turned over to the police or forced to return home. They are given the opportunity to consider alternatives under the supervision of trained counselors. Such a home may need to serve also as a narcotic halfway house. The program may need to include a transportation service to pick up youth who call in for help. Such an operation has obvious risks. Young people may try to use the house merely as a free place to stay. Others may try to use it as a hiding place from police authorities. But churches must take some risks in working with alienated and hostile youth.

Hostel for Transient Youth

Young people traveling for education or pleasure or those newly arrived in a city for work often need clean, inexpensive, safe housing. In some areas the YMCA and the YWCA fill this need. But often there is a lack of adequate facilities. Some churches feel that they can minister to youth by having hostel arrangements for them. Some of these are convertible to other uses during the day and serve merely as sleeping quarters at night. Ideally, facilities for sleeping, bathing, and eating should be furnished. The young people can clean and care for the facilities to keep costs low.

Hot Lunch Program

The aged and the poor often lack money for well-balanced meals. A church can help meet the need for an adequate diet by providing a hot lunch program in the church. By utilizing church kitchens, volunteer help, and food bought in large quantities the cost of meals can be kept low. The operation should be nonprofit with only enough charge to cover the actual cost of operation. Meals should be accompanied by a fellowship period, recreation, and perhaps light entertainment. This not only provides fellowship and recreation but also makes the people feel that this is more than a soup kitchen operation.

Housing Improvement

An acute need in many cities and rural areas is low-cost decent housing. Churches can help provide such housing. The most common way is for a church to form a nonprofit corporation, secure a government loan, and build the housing. This approach, while meeting immediate need, has a number of long-range difficulties. There is question about the church-state relationships involved. Also, it puts a church in the housing business with all of the built-in possibilities for animosity between landlord and tenant. A better approach is for a church to stimulate the forming of a community-wide nonprofit corporation which serves as the holding agent and operator of the housing project. The church would maintain no long-range relationship except to furnish services, such as Bible study, recreation, and counseling. A third approach is for a church to form a nonprofit corporation to purchase, renovate, and sell old houses at the lowest possible price. A fourth technique is for a ministry group to work with persons in substandard housing to improve their facilities. Such a group could serve as a clearinghouse for volunteer skilled and unskilled labor in renovation projects. The concept calls for working *with* the people in the housing, not doing cleanup jobs for them. If the housing is rental property, the owners' permission must be secured. Unless there is a clear understanding beforehand, the owner may raise the rent when the property is improved. His justification for this may be that the improvement raises his taxes and he must make up the difference in higher rent. An appeal should be made to the city not to raise taxes if the owner agrees not to increase the rent.

Another approach is for churches to form ministry groups to work with renters in gaining improvements from landlords. Often a church group can act as a go-between. Such groups should strive to work out as just a settlement as possible. If landlords are making exorbitant profits while not maintaining property, legal action may be called for.

Landlords should meet housing codes.

Finally, a church can provide a service by keeping track of decent low-cost housing and putting those searching for housing in contact with it. A church task force could specialize in housing, keeping abreast of developments in government-subsidized housing programs and private efforts to develop decent housing for low income families. For further information contact the Office of Church and Housing, Board of National Missions, The United Presbyterian Church in the USA, 475 Riverside Dr., New York, N. Y. 10027; The National Urban Coalition, 2100 M St., N.W., Washington, D. C. 20037; and local federal housing authorities.

International Club

Where internationals concentrate there is an opportunity for ministry through an international center or club. Here internationals can gather, have access to recreational equipment, and be able to secure snacks at reasonable cost. The center can also provide tutoring in English, special help in academic courses, and instruction on American history and culture. For those interested in becoming American citizens, classes in citizenship can be offered. Such a center can be part of a church building or can be a separate facility leased and operated by a church or by a cluster of churches. It is important to have workers present to talk with the internationals and help them with problems. Many internationals are in the United States for extended periods of time away from their families. They are often lonely and homesick. They need someone who cares for them and with whom they can talk. In conjunction with an international club, host families can invite internationals into their homes for visits, meals, and trips. For further information see the *Mission Action Group Guide: Internationals,* Woman's Missionary Union, Southern Baptist Convention.

Kindergarten

In some areas public school kindergartens are not available. Churches can fill a ministry role by providing kindergartens. Church kindergartens should have the plus factor of spiritual concern and Bible study. They must also in every way meet the highest standards for excellence in kindergarten level education. The state department of education can supply information on kindergarten programs and state regulations affecting them.

Legal Aid

Many persons of low income do not feel they can afford legal advice. Because they lack such advice they often fall prey to dishonest businesses. Churches can form a task force of Christian lawyers to staff free or low-cost legal centers for persons of low income. Such centers could give legal aid for a variety of problems —those arrested, threatened with legal action by landlords, or involved with loan sharks, for example. The center needs to be located conveniently for persons of low income. It should also be well advertised. Contact a Christian attorney about the steps in estabishing such a program.

Library

A church library can be a vital part of ministry. The library can supply materials for training persons in ministry. It can also distribute materials to persons in need of ministry. It can be a means of general education for persons who have little access to books or who are intimidated by city or university libraries. In underprivileged neighborhoods, aggressive library programs can teach children to value and use books. An adequate library should have not only books, but also tracts and pamphlets. A filing system can store helpful information on particular ministry needs. Such a file is a valuable resource for committees grappling with problems trying to come up with specific ministry programs.

Literacy Training

Many persons are severely handicapped by functional illiteracy. Local churches can provide literacy training. Literacy training centers are found in most metropolitan areas. But literacy materials are accessible to anyone. Persons within the church can be trained in literacy techniques. Then they can teach persons in need to read and to write. The facilities of the church or other facilities convenient to the nonreader can be utilized. Materials used in literacy programs can be obtained from Lit-Lit, 475 Riverside Dr., New York, N. Y. 10027, or from Laubach Literacy, Inc., Box 131, Syracuse, N. Y. 13210. Also see the *Mission Action Group Guide: Nonreaders,* Woman's Missionary Union, Southern Baptist Convention.

Loan Fund for Recently Released Prisoners

Released prisoners face many obstacles in adjusting to normal life. One of these is lack of money to take care of rent, food, and clothing while they look for a job and permanent residence. Churches can provide loan funds to recently released prisoners to carry them through this transition period. The loans being repaid keep the fund alive and money available for others. For further information see the *Mission Action Group Guide: Prisoner Rehabilitation,* Brotherhood Commission, Southern Baptist Convention.

Mass Communication

Mass communication can play an effective role in ministry. Ads in newspapers, radio announcements, and television commercials can let the public know what services the church offers. In addition, churches can provide helpful information to the public via mass media. For example, they can offer consumer advice, warn about frauds, set forth public health news, build a helping community spirit, attack racist ideas, undermine myths which many Americans hold that short-circuit effective social action, and present tips for successful family life.

Several opportunities are open for churches in utilizing mass media. Many newspapers will print well written stories in the public interest. If the stories cannot be printed free, advertisements can be purchased. Television time is extremely expensive and should be used only by persons who have professional competency. Radio is much less expensive and reaches a wide audience. Churches can prepare materials for the public service time on radio, purchase time, or operate their own radio station. Special conferences and programs can be taped and offered to radio stations for use. A television series of wide potential interest can be offered to television stations. They often will produce such programs as a public service.

One way to effectively utilize mass media is to develop a mass media ministries team composed of persons who are skilled in public relations, writing, and advertising. Such persons know the procedure for the proper use of mass media. They are also skilled in writing copy.

Meal-on-Wheels Program

Many people are confined to homes and unable to go out for meals or to cook their own. The chronically ill, handicapped, and the aged living alone are in special need of at least one hot nourishing meal a day. The meal-on-wheels program is designed to furnish such meals. Usually, the meals are prepared in a central kitchen, placed in vehicles with equipment to keep the food hot, and delivered. The cost of these meals can be kept low by buying the food in large quantities, using church kitchens, and utilizing volunteer help. Retired persons and women whose children no longer live at home are prime prospects for staffing such a program.

Medical and Dental Care

Adequate medical care is often difficult for the poor to obtain. They lack funds and frequently transportation to take them to medical centers. Churches can meet these needs in a number of ways. Utilizing physicians and nurses who volunteer their time and drugs donated by pharmacies and drug companies, a church can operate an efficient, low-cost clinic in its facilities. Several churches operate well-baby clinics offering checkups for babies and child-care education for mothers. Other clinics are for the sick and accept patients from all ages. Some congregations maintain a clinic apart from the church plant. Churches in middle class or high income neighborhoods may establish a clinic in a low income neighborhood. It may be in a mission or in a facility rented or owned for the purpose of a medical clinic. A mobile clinic is another possibility. A mobile unit equipped for medical and dental care and staffed by volunteer physicians and nurses can be driven into areas of high medical need. Such a unit can also be used for health education. A church can also provide free medical checkups by physicians and dentists. Whenever a medical or dental need is discovered, an appointment is made with a cooperating physician or dentist who supplies the needed medical attention at little or no cost. For further information see *How to Begin the Church Community Clinic Program* from the Direct Missions Department, Baptist General Convention of Texas, Baptist Building, Dallas, Texas 75201.

Mom's Day/Night Out

For their own emotional health as well as the stability of their family, mothers need time away from children. Churches can perform a ministry by providing a place for children to be left while

mothers shop, go to the beauty parlor, visit with friends, or do whatever helps relieve tension. Such services can be provided in the
church's nursery and elementary facilities. A church can make a
small charge for the service or operate it free by utilizing cooperative
volunteer workers. Such a program can be operated in conjunction
with day-care programs, short-term child-care programs for mothers
engaged in church ministry, and normal church nursery operations.

Multiple Ministries in Shopping Centers

Shopping centers provide an excellent location for ministry. Persons
from all walks of life come to shopping centers. Here their time is
less structured than at work, recreation, or home. A ministry in a
shopping center can be located in a separate nearby building or in
space leased from the center. Although such a ministry can be
supported by a single church, there is advantage in this being a
cooperative ministry among several churches. It can be staffed by
volunteers or by full-time paid staff members. The following ministries have been carried out by marketplace ministries: (1) A
shoppers' child-care center where children can be left by parents who
are shopping. Children are given excellent care and guidance by trained
staff personnel. With volunteer workers the charge for such service
can be minimal. (2) A preschool program. Such a program can
serve people who live in the neighborhood surrounding the marketplace as well as those who work in the stores. The school can be run
in conjunction with the hourly child-care program but as a separate
entity. (3) A housing service. Trained consultants can be on duty
to help people locate suitable housing. (4) Art exhibits. The
marketplace ministry center is an excellent place to exhibit art. The
art can be by persons involved in classes and art centers sponsored
by the marketplace ministry. (5) Telephone referral. This ministry
provides a center where persons can call to get specific information
or help. Trained consultants help persons with specific requests, such
as emergency babysitting, transportation, location of psychiatric help,
and other matters. (6) Counseling. A center can maintain a staff
counselor and also refer persons to other counselors. Referral service
should be provided for pastoral care, psychiatric care, and psychologi-
cal counseling. The center should keep a list of persons who are
available to give needed counsel. In addition, people should be available to provide transportation for those needing it to get to a trained

counselor. (7) Discussions and lectures. Lectures and discussions on topics of wide concern can be presented daily. Such discussions or lectures could be on child care, successful retirement, managing money, health, spiritual problems, depression, loneliness, emotional crises, marital strife, and many others. A many-faceted program requires numerous volunteers. These can come from churches surrounding the shopping center. Churches should make available material describing their programs and inviting people to become involved in the church.

Music

Music can play an effective role in the church's program of ministry. Choirs, voice lessons, instrumental training, bands, and bell choirs give many people hours of enjoyment and a sense of worth. Music for special groups has therapy value. Retired persons frequently find choir groups a meaningful experience, especially when combined with travel. Music therapy for retarded and mentally ill persons has proved effective. Outdoor music festivals are an effective way of enlisting community interest and bearing evangelistic witness. Trained music groups can serve in many ministry functions, such as entertaining in institutions, providing programs for community activities, and performing for benefits. Homes for the aged, mental hospitals, institutions for retarded children, and prisons are often open for music programs by church groups.

Neighborhood Improvement Organization

A church can minister to its community by helping organize a neighborhood improvement program. Although the church itself cannot carry out such a program, it can be the key factor in establishing an organization to do so. The purpose of a community organization is to survey the community, discover needs, and develop specific programs for action. A community organization may involve housing projects, community centers, special education projects, job training, improvement of sanitary facilities, and other similar activities. A neighborhood improvement organization is usually made up of various churches, businesses, and private groups in the community.

Newcomer Service

People moving into a community for the first time often need help in many ways. A church can minister to these persons. A newcomer ministry team composed of persons who have a knack of meeting strangers, making them feel comfortable, and assuring them of the sincerity of offers for help, can carry out this ministry. Many cities have newcomer services, but these seldom relate to a church. Lists of newcomers are obtainable from newcomer services in some cities and from utility companies in others. A printed form can be used by visitors to leave names, addresses, phone numbers, and other information about people, services, and organizations the newcomer will probably need. The form should be drawn up suitable for the neighborhood in which the church is located. Each church will want to devise its own particular form. Here is a suggestion:

Welcome

Welcome to your new home. Since moving can often leave a person wondering where to turn for help, let me recommend the following as my personal suggestions to tide you over until you locate your own:

	Name	Address	Telephone
Physician			
Dentist			
Sitter			
Mechanic			
Plumber			
Electrician			

Also, please call on my church if we can help in any way—The First Baptist Church, 100 Main Street, 822-4666.

I. M. Christian   4300 Way Street   123-4567

Personal Grooming for the Needy

Many either cannot afford such things as haircuts and beauty treatments or are unable to go to barber shops or beauty shops. Churches can minister to such persons by making these personal grooming services available. For those who are confined to homes or institutions, ministering teams can make house or institution calls. For individuals unable to afford these services, the church can establish a grooming center in which volunteers give haircuts and beauty treatments. These centers can also be places where Christian literature is available and personal witness is given. Some feel that a charge should be made for these services. Although the charge is small, it helps the person to maintain his self-respect. Others believe that the service should be offered free.

Personnel Resource File

Community agencies and individuals often need persons with specific skills to volunteer their time for projects. A church can minister by maintaining a central record system of persons who have particular skills and who are willing to give time in a volunteer capacity for community agencies, church programs, and the meeting of human need. The ideal way to operate such a service is with a computer. A computer can be used to store information about an individual. When a request is made, the information can be pulled rapidly and given to the one making the request. A key to the effectiveness of the program is to constantly solicit volunteers and to check the records frequently to make certain that the information is correct and up to date. One means of securing data is to survey church members asking them to check on a card their skills, time available for ministry, and other related information. These cards can be prepared for use with a computer. See Appendix C for a sample of such a survey form.

Planned Parenthood Clinic

In poverty areas where medical care is limited and families are often larger, planned parenthood clinics can be part of a ministries program. Such clinics can be operated in the church or in other buildings supported by the church. They can be operated by church personnel or by persons involved in community planned parenthood programs. The clinics usually function best when staffed by people from the community rather than by outsiders. The clinics usually provide birth control information, hold conferences on the advantage of planned parenthood, and distribute contraceptive materials. The services are either free or inexpensive. For information on establishing a clinic contact Planned Parenthood centers in your city or Planned Parenthood-World Population, 515 Madison Avenue, New York, New York   10022.

Prenatal Care and Counsel

Medical authorities stress the importance of prenatal care for the health and well-being of a child. Churches can help with prenatal care through several types of ministry. One is education and counsel for the expectant mother. Another involves food for an adequate diet, medical care, and counseling to deal with emotional problems. A program can be mainly one of education. In areas where medical care is inadequate, diets are substandard, and mothers often are unaware of what is involved in prenatal care, a church will have to take added steps. If a church operates a medical clinic program, prenatal care and counseling can be made available and doctors can give counsel. Some clinics offer special courses in prenatal care offered by volunteer workers in conjunction with the medical program. Others utilize home visitation to talk with expectant mothers about the need for prenatal care. The food center can provide items for a balanced diet. Necessary vitamins and adequate protein should be made available to all women who are pregnant. The Public Health Service, physicians, and nurses can provide information for prenatal care programs.

Preschool Program

The preschool program is distinct from child care. It is a program of child development and education for children ages three, four, and five. Many find that a morning session for one group of children and an afternoon session for another works well. The preschool program is not designed for children of working parents, but for those whose parents can bring them in the morning and pick them up at noon or bring them at noon and pick them up in late afternoon. The preschool program needs to be designated for the age level of the child and adjusted to the circumstances in which the child lives. A preschool program in a rural area will not be the same as one for an inner city. One for a three-year-old will not be the same as one for a four- or five-year-old. Check local ordinances and regulations governing a preschool program. Certain standards must be maintained.

Recreation

Recreation programs can be carried out by churches to meet the needs of many different groups and persons. The recreation supplied should fit the persons involved. A program for elementary children after school should not be the same as one for retired senior citizens. Some churches construct special facilities for recreation, such as church gymnasiums, bowling alleys, and swimming pools. Others utilize parking lots and open playgrounds. Important to all is adequate supervision. In the larger programs, full-time paid staff members direct the activities. In most cases, volunteers do the work.

Certain individuals are especially benefited by recreation. Children whose parents work are helped by after-school recreation. The aged and retired appreciate planned leisuretime activities. The mentally retarded and handicapped benefit from recreation programs planned especially for them. Single adults need fellowship and recreation.

Recreation Clinics

The natural human interest in play coupled with added leisure time makes recreation a prime means of ministry. In addition to recreation programs, churches can hold clinics in which they teach people how to play and how to direct others in play. People will respond especially well to such clinics if they are staffed by well-known athletes. For example, a church can hold a clinic in basketball using the local basketball stars to teach it. The same can be done for other sports—golf, fishing, hunting, tennis, bowling, and many others.

Remedial Reading Program

Children frequently have difficulty in reading. Churches can minister by providing remedial reading programs, tutoring services, and special study halls. The most difficult of these, and perhaps the most needed, is the remedial program. The church can form a team of remedial reading teachers, provide them with up-to-date training, and establish times and places for them to meet with students. The program can be operated after school or on weekends. It can also function as a summer school program.

Rent and Utility Assistance

Often families find themselves unable to pay rent or utility bills. A church can minister through a task force trained to work with people in such need. The task force can negotiate with landlords about an extension of time for payment of rent, sometimes guaranteeing the rent. It can perform a similar service with utility companies. If the church pays the rent or utilities, the person should repay the amount when able. Repayment enables the church to provide emergency assistance to others in similar need.

Resort Leisure Ministry

An increasing number of persons go to resort areas, parks, and public beaches. Many possibilities exist for ministries in such places. Mobile units for worship services, Bible study, and discussion groups can be utilized to cover several different resort areas in a common geographic region. Permanent chapels with counseling centers can be erected in places with large numbers of vacationers or weekend dwellers. Christian entertainment can be supplied. Singing, drama, comedy acts, and other church-sponsored activities can be coupled with Christian testimony and invitations to participate in worship and Bible study. For further information see *Mission Action Group Guide: Resort Areas,* Brotherhood Commission, Southern Baptist Convention.

Roving Street Minister

A trained minister roving the streets can meet many needs. Such a person ought to be sensitive to human hurt, courageous, and able to size up a situation and act decisively. He should also be familiar with resources for referral. He can visit bars, gambling casinos, areas where strip shows and burlesque houses are common, homosexual centers, red light districts, and neighborhoods noted for violence. If a person becomes known in an area for his genuine concern, people will go to him when they are in trouble. His tasks will include counseling, referral services, arbitrating disputes, stimulating consciences, and providing emergency medical care. For further information read *Night Pastors* by Stanley Matthew and *The Church Creative* edited by M. Edward Clark and others, pages 104-8.

Scholarships for Youth from Poverty Areas

Breaking the cycle of poverty is difficult. One of the ways to help do it is through education. But students from poor homes are at a disadvantage in securing adequate education. Often they require not only encouragement but also financial assistance. Some youth drop out of high school because they feel they cannot afford to pay for the normal activities of high school. Many don't go to college because they don't have enough money. Although numerous scholarships are available, they are frequently restricted to particular groups of people. Furthermore, many poor families do not know the procedure for securing scholarships. And there are not enough scholarships to go around. A church, therefore, can minister by providing scholarship funds for qualified students and encouraging them to pursue higher education. Churches in poverty areas may need to secure funds for such a program from more affluent churches. Churches with middle and upper class members can link with a poor church to supply funds for scholarships. A group of qualified persons should supervise the program. The group should initiate discussion with qualified students. Because a disproportionate number of Negroes are both poor and lacking in education, such scholarships ought to concentrate on black students.

School for Excluded Children

In the inner city and transition communities some children are excluded from public schools. A number are classified as retarded or uneducable. Others are declared to be social misfits. Often these children need only special care and attention. In some instances counseling and psychiatric help are called for. Public schools often do not have these helps available. Churches located in areas where such needs are concentrated can minister by providing a school for excluded children. This would be distinct from a child-care center or from a preschool center. It would major on children usually termed "problem children." It requires teachers especially trained in working with such children. The hope is that many of the children will be so helped that they will be able to enter the public school programs. Others may need to be referred to schools for the retarded or to institutional care. The school will more than likely major on younger children since these are the ones most often excluded. Older children would be included in programs for school dropouts.

Senior Citizens' Lounge

The aging need an easily accessible place to meet, have recreation, and eat. A church can minister by providing such a place. It should be on the street level near an outside entrance reached without steps or long walks. Such a room need not be elaborate. But it should be bright and attractive. There should be such things as a snack bar, games, reading material, a television set, conversation centers, a telephone, and some special equipment, such as books in large type, books on tape, and earphones for stereos and television sets which can be adjusted volume-wise for the needs of the listener. This room could also be used for Bible study, devotional programs, and special meetings. The following books provide hints for such a senior citizens' lounge: *Older Members of the Congregation* by Arthur Rismiller, *Mission Action Group Guide: The Aging* by the Woman's Missionary Union, Southern Baptist Convention, *The Church Creative* edited by Jim Edward Clark and others.

Sex Education Program

In numerous communities there is no adequate sex education. The families do not do an adequate job, the public schools are harrassed if they try, and many churches have neglected this phase of human life. As a result, there is widespread confusion and harm. Churches can provide a better sex education program than any other institution. The concept of sex as a gift of God enables a church to put sex in a perspective different from that of a secular institution. A church can stress that sex is part of man's total life and is related to his spiritual well-being. Sex education conferences can be part of the Church Training program, church camps, special conferences, and counseling sessions. Qualified counselors, Christian physicians, and trained staff members can conduct these sessions. The Concordia sex education series, available in book stores, is excellent for use in churches. The "Sexuality in Christian Living" series published by Broadman is recommended for personal and home use.

Shopping for the Handicapped

People who are handicapped and live alone frequently find shopping difficult, especially shopping for groceries. They can order clothing, household goods, and medicine through mail order catalogs and over the phone. But few grocery stores offer any kind of delivery service. A ministry team can take the shopping list of the handicapped, purchase the groceries, and deliver them. The list could either be called in to a church or picked up by a member of the team.

Sisters Program

The daughters of mothers receiving aid to dependent children frequently receive similar aid when they become mothers. In order to try to break this cycle, a church can pair ADC mothers with non-ADC mothers in discussion and conference groups. Through group therapy, friendship, and encouragement the children in ADC homes could be exposed to another way of life. And the ADC mothers could gain some sense of self-respect.

Small Group Foster Care

Large institutional care for children is considered inadequate. The number of individual foster homes is limited. An in-between approach is to provide small-group foster care. In such a program a small number of children live in one house with house parents who serve as their foster parents. A church can minister by providing a house and foster parents. In some situations the foster parents are paid a full-time salary to care for the children. In others the man has a job outside of the home. The cost of the latter plan is less and in some ways provides a more normal homelife. Contact the Child Welfare Unit in your county for information on foster home care or write the state Department of Public Welfare.

Big Brother, Big Sister Programs

The big brother and big sister programs match a needy boy or girl with a sponsoring adult man or woman. The basic concept is one of friendship, guidance, and support in times of crisis. Churches can operate such a program with special ministry teams or they can invite already established big brother or big sister programs into the church. For further information contact Big Brothers of America, 341 Suburban Station Building, Philadelphia, Pennsylvania 19103.

Staff Members for Ministry

The ministry programs of a church deserve skilled, professional guidance. Such programs rank in importance with those for education and music, both of which have enjoyed full-time staff leadership in many churches for years. A number of churches now employ staff members to direct efforts to meet human need. Some of these staff members are trained both in theology and social work. Others are skilled in special areas of ministry, such as work with the aged. Still others major in counseling. A minister of ministries is responsible for enlisting personnel, supervising programs, acting as a source of information, and being alert to referral opportunities. He should become an integral part of the ministry of the community as well as of the total program of the church.

Study Hall

In many neighborhoods, especially poverty areas, homes are seldom suitable for study. People are crammed into few rooms, the walls are thin, the noise level is intense. In order for children to have a suitable place to study, churches can minister by providing a study hall. It needs to be in a place which is well lighted, equipped with desks, and supervised to provide reasonable quiet. Basic reference books such as dictionaries and encyclopedias should be available. A tutoring program can be combined with the study hall. Students may become dependent on tutors to do homework. Therefore, it is imperative that trained, skilled workers be utilized.

Teen Center

Nondestructive recreation for young people is lacking in many areas. A church can minister by providing a place for youth to gather, talk, play games, and snack. Churches often turn basements or entire houses into teen centers. Teen centers should be planned and decorated by the young people. The center should provide activities which interest young people and which cannot only entertain them but also help them deal with basic problems. A teen center provides a place young people can call their own. They can meet without the constant presence of overly concerned adults or the pressures by peers toward harmful acts.

Telephone Checkup Service

Persons who live alone need frequent contact with others. This is especially true of the aged and the handicapped. Sudden illness or accident can prevent a person's reaching help. In order to allow these people to feel more secure, a daily, or even more frequent, telephone checkup can be operated by a church. A list of persons needing this service with their phone numbers is used by a telephone ministries group. The persons on the list are called at specified intervals. If there is no answer, a visit is made to see if something is wrong. This is a ministry which can be performed by those who are themselves confined. The blind, the orthopedically handicapped, mothers with small children, and the aged who live with others are excellent prospects for carrying out such a ministry.

Telephone Counseling and Referral

An increasingly common ministry is a telephone center for counseling and referral. In such a program a church staffs a center with volunteers who answer calls, talk with persons about their problems, make referrals, and sometimes dispatch emergency ministry teams. The volunteers usually work no more than three or four hours, but someone mans the telephone twenty-four hours a day. The telephone number is widely advertised. The key to success in such a program involves two factors: (1) the careful training of the volunteers and (2) adequate resources for referral. Most successful centers maintain an extensive file of particular problems and community resources for meeting those problems. An added feature is to have a number of persons standing by ready to give immediate aid in response to particular problems. For example, a group could be called upon to provide transportation in emergencies. A domestic care group could provide home care in an emergency. A suicide prevention team could be available for dispatch to persons threatening suicide. A group of people skilled in working with alcoholics could be on call to go immediately to an alcoholic who calls for help. For further information see *As Close as the Telephone* by Alan Walker.

Thrift Store

Many persons are unwilling to accept charity clothing and furniture. However, they will respond to a bargain. A thrift store is a place where people can purchase used clothing, furniture, and household appliances for a fraction of their original cost. All items in the store are to be clean, reasonably in style, and operating. The store is frequently staffed by volunteers to keep the cost down. Items in the store are contributed. This means that all merchandise can be sold for very little. The Salvation Army and Goodwill Industries maintain thrift store operations and can supply helpful information.

Town Hall Discussions

In a former era church buildings frequently served as the meeting place for citizens to discuss community issues. Today such meetings are held infrequently. But there is still need for the airing of views on community issues. And the church building is still a valid place in which to meet. A church can sponsor meetings at which various viewpoints are expressed on issues related to the community. The person presiding should be skilled in making discussions constructive rather than destructive and in controlling conflict. It should be clear that no vote will be taken, no resolutions passed, and no action initiated at the meeting. The purpose is informational. Individuals may become concerned enough in the meeting to form themselves into action groups. But the purpose of the meeting is to give people an opportunity to discuss significant issues in an open, honest way.

Training in Community Services

Most churches have few members who know what resources are available to help persons in need. This inadequacy handicaps a referral ministry. By offering classes in community resources a church not only will strengthen its own ministries program but also equip persons from other churches and community offices. People who know community resources can be utilized in a telephone ministry referral service as well as in the counseling operation of the church. They can also help staff inner-city ministry centers, rescue missions, and community services programs.

Training Program for Ministry

Some churches have professional persons as members who can train workers for ministry programs. A church with social workers, lawyers, schoolteachers, counselors, and psychologists, for example, can run a continuing training program for ministry. Examples of classes which can be offered are: community resources and referral, counseling, tutoring, literacy, day care, preschool, and health education.

Transportation

Transportation is needed by many—the poor, the handicapped, the aged. Churches can minister by providing such transportation. Most public and private transportation is ill-equipped to carry persons with physical handicaps. Individuals on crutches can make it on and off most busses and subways. But persons in wheelchairs are stranded. Church-supplied transportation can consist of busses or vans equipped with lifts or ramps. The handicapped or aged person can be loaded onto the vehicle and off again without his having to leave a wheelchair or climb steps. Persons confined to institutions for the aged can be transported to medical centers, shopping areas, and churches. The poor can be provided transportation to doctors and work. Many churches now have fleets of busses used only on Sunday which could be put into service seven days a week.

Tutoring

Many children need tutoring. Some are slow learners. Others have family situations which handicap them. A number of churches have established tutoring programs for such children. The programs are usually operated in conjunction with after school clubs and recreation activities. But the tutoring program can stand on its own. Most have found it advisable to consult with the public schools in establishing the ministry. Retired teachers, mothers, and older skilled students are those most often used for tutors. In the most successful programs, pupils are picked up after school, brought to the church, and taken home following the tutoring session. For further information see *How to Begin the Church Community Tutoring Program,* Direct Missions Department, Baptist General Convention of Texas, Baptist Building, Dallas, Texas   75201.

Visitation of the Confined

People confined to their home or an institution frequently require special ministry. Some are confined by illness or age. Others are forcibly restrained, such as those in jails, prisons, mental hospitals, homes for the retarded, and institutions for juvenile offenders. Others are in institutions voluntarily but are not able to move about freely, such as those in homes for unwed mothers, narcotic and alcohol rehabilitation centers, and halfway houses. Confined persons need visits and opportunities for conversation with concerned individuals. Visitors in a ministry program should participate in a training program to learn how to visit, what to say, how long to stay, what sort of follow-up to make, and how to relate the individual to other persons. Visitors can perform a number of services, such as buying requested items and delivering them, mailing letters, writing letters, reading to persons who aren't able to read, and seeking specialized assistance when needed. These visits will afford many opportunities for spiritual guidance and witness. The following materials have helpful information on visitation: *Mission Action Group Guide: The Sick,* Woman's Missionary Union, Southern Baptist Convention.

Vocational Training

The need for vocational training is great in many areas. Churches help in job training several ways. Some operate what amounts to trade schools using skilled personnel in the church to teach classes in such things as automobile mechanics, typing, shorthand, filing, and bookkeeping. Others are offering their facilities to government and nonprofit private groups for vocational training. In some areas it might be possible for a church to utilize business facilities in off hours for training. For example, a garage might turn over its facilities at night to a skilled mechanic and a class in order that he could have adequate facilities for teaching mechanics. A business might allow a class and teacher to use its offices for training in typing, dictation, filing, switchboard operation, and other similar jobs. In order to be fully effective, a job training program needs to be coupled with a placement program.

Weight Reducing and Exercise Programs

Numerous Americans suffer from overweight and lack of exercise. Since the Bible indicates God's concern about physical well-being, a church ministry can be directed toward proper weight and exercise. Some churches are able to supply elaborate facilities such as gymnasiums and exercise rooms. Others are able only to afford exercise in athletic programs, games on the parking lot, or a makeshift exercise room. Weight reducing programs can include group therapy. In such groups those struggling to lose weight reinforce each other's determination. The church library can supply books on exercise, diet, and health.

Youth Service Corps

Churches are finding that young people want not simply to be entertained but also to serve. Providing opportunities for service in keeping with the skills and abilities of youth is a challenging task. The youth service corps could provide personnel for a number of different types of ministries: recreation for neglected children after school, summer recreation-crafts-Bible study for children in underprivileged areas, visitation and recreation in homes for the aged, renovation of substandard housing, volunteer nurses' aides in clinics, baby sitting services, short-term child care, tutoring of younger children, literacy training, consultants in telephone referral ministries, sorting of clothes for a clothing center, serving as a clerk in a clothing center, food center, or thrift store, fixing food and waiting on tables in a coffeehouse, working in a church library, teaching citizenship classes, child care and education for the children of migrant workers, directing athletic programs, teaching classes in art, crafts, and hobbies, camping for younger children, helping with preschool breakfasts, working with a headliners group in locating persons in need, entertainment and recreation for the institutionalized, supplying emergency domestic help, interpreting for the deaf, conducting services in the jail, and constructing furniture and equipment for the various ministry programs.

IV

Resources for Ministry

The following provide helpful resources for programs of ministry and application. The listings are selected from a large body of material. They are from many different points of view. No one will agree with all they say. Yet all supply useful insights. The resources are listed in three categories: books, periodicals, and organizations.

Books

Belew, M. Wendell. *Churches and How They Grow*. Nashville: Broadman Press, 1971. Descriptions of innovative church programs. Emphasis on multiple ministry approach.

The Church and Community Survey Workbook. Nashville: Convention Press, 1970. Contains step-by-step procedure which a church can use to survey the needs of its surrounding community. Available at Baptist Book Stores.

Church Community Weekday Ministries. Department of Christian Social Ministries. Atlanta: Home Mission Board of the Southern Baptist Convention. A brief pamphlet listing over sixty different types of ministries and setting forth a few simple steps or procedures.

Delamarter, Walter. *The Diakonic Task*. Atlanta: Home Mission Board, Southern Baptist Convention, 1970. By a man trained in theology, psychology, and social work. Sets forth the biblical concept of servanthood and what this means today.

Dittes, James E. *The Church in the Way*. New York: Scribner's, 1967. A very carefully worked out case for the relevance of the church and ministry. Helpful insights on turning conflict, resistance, and meandering into positive, creative channels.

Edge, Findley B. *The Greening of the Church*. Waco, Texas: Word Books, 1971. A theological and practical discussion of the mission of the people of God with an emphasis on ministry.

Etzioni, Amitai and Eva, eds. *Social Change: Sources, Patterns, and*

Consequences. New York: Basic Books, 1964. A collection of writings showing the basic theories of social change.

Fisher, Wallace E. *Preface to Parish Renewal: A Study Guide for Laymen.* Nashville: Abingdon Press, 1968. A practical guidebook for laymen in renewal by a pastor who has experience in church renewal.

Geyer, Nancy, and Noll, Shirley. *Team Building in Church Groups.* Valley Forge: Judson Press, 1970. Helpful for organizing "Task Forces," "Work Groups," and "Mission Groups," the basic structures of many programs of ministry and application in local churches.

Goodman, Grace Ann. *Rocking the Ark.* New York: Presbyterian Distribution Service, 1969. Nine case studies of congregations of from 100 to 3,000 members in rural, downtown, and suburban locations. Discusses how conflict in each situation was handled.

Greenwood, Elma L. *How Churches Fight Poverty: 60 Successful Local Projects.* New York: Friendship Press, 1967. A series of case studies of ministry projects and antipoverty programs.

Henderson, Lloyd. *How to Begin the Church Community Clinic Program.* Booklet prepared and distributed by the Direct Missions Department, Baptist General Convention of Texas, Baptist Building, Dallas, Texas 75201. A brief practical guide for setting up clinic programs, complete with case histories.

Henderson, Lloyd. *How to Begin the Church Community Tutoring Program.* Booklet prepared and distributed by the Direct Missions Department, Baptist General Convention of Texas, Baptist Building, Dallas, Texas 75201. A brief, practical guide on setting up tutoring programs.

Henderson, Lloyd. *How to Begin the Church Day Care Ministry.* Booklet prepared and distributed by the Direct Missions Department, Baptist General Convention of Texas, Baptist Building, Dallas, Texas 75201. A brief practical guide for a general program of weekday ministries.

Henderson, Lloyd. *How to Begin the Church Weekday Clubs Ministry.* Booklet prepared and distributed by the Direct Missions Department, Baptist General Convention of Texas, Baptist Building, Dallas, Texas 75201. Practical suggestions on establishing a club program for youth, mothers, and the aged.

Hessell, Dieter T. *Reconciliation and Conflict.* Philadelphia: Westminster Press, 1969. An analysis of controversy in the churches over social action and suggestions on what to do about it. Basically sympathetic with social action by churches.

Hiltner, Seward. *Ferment in the Ministry.* New York: Abingdon Press, 1969. Brief discussion of new forms of ministry with relation to ministry and application.

Hinson, E. Glenn. *The Church: Design for Survival.* Nashville: Broadman Press, 1967. Discusses basic questions on the nature and function of the church. Suggests new approaches for worship, education, ministry, and social action. Suggestive rather than exhaustive.

Howell, Robert L. *Fish for My People.* New York: Morehouse-Barlow, 1968. Sets forth step-by-step development of a group dedicated to helping people in difficulty. Excellent source.

Knight, Walker L. *Struggle for Integrity.* Waco, Texas: Word Books, 1969. The story of a community church in its effort to minister in a changing community.

Mission Action Group Guide: The Aging. Birmingham: Woman's Missionary Union, Southern Baptist Convention, 1968. Specific suggestions for a church group in ministering to the aging. Resources and other materials listed.

Mission Action Group Guide: Apartment Dwellers. Memphis: Brotherhood Commission, Southern Baptist Convention, 1971. Describes the challenges and opportunities for churches in dealing with apartment dwellers. Includes specific program suggestions and suggested resources.

Mission Action Group Guide: Combating Moral Problems. Memphis: Brotherhood Commission, Southern Baptist Convention, 1968. Practical suggestions on dealing with issues such as alcoholism, sexual problems, pornography, and racism.

Mission Action Group Guide: Economically Disadvantaged. Birmingham: Woman's Missionary Union, Southern Baptist Convention, 1967. Specific programs for ministering to the needs of the poor.

Mission Action Group Guide: Headliners. Birmingham: Woman's Missionary Union, Southern Baptist Convention, 1968. Sets forth suggestions for securing names of persons in need or groups of persons in need by being attentive to news releases.

Mission Action Group Guide: Internationals. Birmingham: Woman's Missionary Union, Southern Baptist Convention, 1967. Specific programs for ministry to internationals.

Mission Action Group Guide: Juvenile Rehabilitation. Birmingham: Woman's Missionary Union, Southern Baptist Convention, 1967. Practical suggestions on group action to minister to juveniles who have serious problems.

Mission Action Group Guide: Language Groups. Birmingham: Woman's Missionary Union, Southern Baptist Convention, 1967. Suggestions for group action in ministering to persons in the United States who speak little or no English, to those who are members of ethnic minorities.

Mission Action Group Guide: Military. Memphis: Brotherhood Commission, Southern Baptist Convention, 1968. Specific program suggestions for ministry to persons involved in military service.

Mission Action Group Guide: Negroes. Memphis: Brotherhood Commission, Southern Baptist Convention, 1968. Practical actions by groups to minister to the special needs of the American Negro.

Mission Action Group Guide: Nonreaders. Birmingham: Woman's Missionary Union, Southern Baptist Convention, 1968. Suggestions for setting up a literacy program.

Mission Action Group Guide: Prisoner Rehabilitation. Memphis: Brotherhood Commission, Southern Baptist Convention, 1968. Specific program ideas for ministering to the prisoner and the released offender.

Mission Action Group Guide: Resort Areas. Memphis: Brotherhood Commission, Southern Baptist Convention, 1968. Programs for groups dealing with ministries to resort centers.

Mission Action Group Guide: The Sick. Birmingham: Woman's Missionary Union, Southern Baptist Convention, 1967: Specific programs for ministering to the sick.

Mission Action Group Guide: A Guide for Mission Action Projects. Birmingham: Woman's Missionary Union, Southern Baptist Convention, 1967. Suggestions for short-term projects of ministry and how to carry them out.

Mission Action Survey Guide. Birmingham: Woman's Missionary Union, Southern Baptist Convention, 1967. Practical plans for discovering community needs through survey.

Moberg, David O. *Inasmuch: Christian Social Responsibility in the Twentieth Century.* Grand Rapids: William B. Eerdmans Pub. Co., 1965. A basic theoretical, theological, and practical book for ministry. Begins with theological statement and moves to practical suggestions for local church action. Excellent source.

Oates, Wayne E. and Neely, Kirk H. *Where to Go for Help*, rev. enl. ed. Philadelphia: Westminster Press, 1972. Helpful on locating resources for ministering to human need.

O'Connor, Elizabeth. *Call to Commitment*. New York: Harper and Row, 1963. The story of the Church of the Savior in Washington, D. C. Task force approach.

O'Connor, Elizabeth. *Journey Inward, Journey Outward*. New York: Harper and Row, 1968. Description of Church of the Savior in Washington, D. C. Describes worship and spiritual exercises for journey inward and some of the programs of ministry in journey outward. Shows need for both *inward* and *outward* involvement.

Palmer, Charles E. *The Church and the Exceptional Person*. New York: Abingdon Press, 1961. How to locate and serve persons with impaired hearing or vision, those who are intellectually gifted or retarded, and the crippled, speech handicapped, emotionally disturbed, institutionalized, home-bound, and multi-handicapped.

Raines, Robert A. *The Secular Congregation*. New York: Harper and Row, 1968. Description of small groups in ministry and social action as well as worship and Bible study.

Reitz, Rudiger. *The Church in Experiment: Studies in New Congregational Structures and Functional Mission*. New York: Abingdon Press, 1969. Describes what is being done in the United States in creative programs of ministry and application. More descriptive than prescriptive. Helpful to introduce a group to new possibilities.

Schaller, Lyle E. *The Impact of the Future*. Nashville: Abingdon Press, 1969. Discusses changes in American life and suggested responses on the part of the church. Very helpful.

Seifert, Harvey. *Power Where the Action Is*. Philadelphia: Westminster Press, 1968. An experienced writer on churches in community action sets forth positive suggestions for dealing with the power structure of society.

Torney, George A., ed. *Toward Creative Urban Strategy*. Waco, Texas: Word Books, 1970. A collection of articles on the church and the city with a strong ministry emphasis.

Trexler, Edgar R., ed. *Ways to Wake Up Your Church*. Philadelphia: Fortress Press, 1969. Specific examples of innovative ministries in different types of churches.

Trueblood, Elton. *The New Man for Our Time*. New York: Harper and Row, 1970. A plea for a balance of pietism and activism.

Walker, Alan. *A Ringing Call to Mission*. New York: Abingdon Press, 1966. A general discussion of the basis for and approach to a church in ministry. Some practical suggestions.

Wirt, Sherwood Eliot. *The Social Conscience of the Evangelical*. New York: Harper and Row, 1968. Effort to bridge the gap between ethics and evangelism by showing that in the best of evangelical thought and practice the two go together.

Periodicals

Christian Century. A nondenominational journal. Editorials and articles on matters of religious, political and social concern. Book reviews and news of the Christian world. W $8.50, $.30 per copy. Christian Century Foundation, 407 S. Dearborn St., Chicago, Ill. 60605.

Christianity Today. Articles, editorials, and news features discuss contemporary events of interest to religious leaders in relation to the underlying theological issues. For clergymen and laymen. BW $5.00. 1014 Washington Bldg., Washington, D. C. 20005.

Church in Mission. Contains frequent examples of churches in ministry and application. Presbyterian. Five times a year. $1.00. 341 Ponce de Leon Ave., N.E., Atlanta, Ga. 30308.

Faith at Work. Discusses application of Christian faith to life. Six times a year. $5.00. 1000 Century Plaza, Suite 210, Columbia, Md. 21043.

Home Missions. Publication of Home Mission Board of the Southern Baptist Convention. Frequent articles on churches in ministry. M $1.50. 1350 Spring St., N.W., Atlanta, Ga. 30309.

Presbyterian Survey. Contains case studies and articles on ministry and action projects. M. 341 Ponce de Leon Ave., N.E., Atlanta, Ga. 30308.

Organizations

Board for Social Welfare Ministry and World Relief, Lutheran Church — Missouri Synod, 210 N. Broadway, St. Louis, Mo. 63102.

Board of Social Ministry, Lutheran Church in America, 231 Madison

Ave., New York, N. Y.   10016.

Department of Christian Action and Community Service, Disciples of Christ, 222 S. Downey Ave., Indianapolis, Ind.   46219.

Division of Christian Life and Mission, National Council of Churches, 475 Riverside Dr., New York, N. Y.   10027.

Executive Council of the Episcopal Church, 815 Second Ave., New York, N. Y.   10017.

General Board of Christian Social Concerns of the United Methodist Church, 100 Maryland Ave., N.E., Washington, D. C.   20002.

Home Mission Board, Southern Baptist Convention, 1350 Spring St., N.W., Atlanta, Ga.   30309.

National Association of Evangelicals, Social Concern Commission, 1405 G. St., N.W., Washington, D. C.   20005.

National Division, Board of Mission, The United Methodist Church, 475 Riverside Dr., New York, N. Y.   10027.

United Church Board for Homeland Ministries, United Church of Christ, 287 Park Ave., S., New York, N. Y.   10010.

United Presbyterian Church in the USA, Board of National Missions, 475 Riverside Dr., New York, N. Y.   10027.

U. S. Catholic Conference, 1312 Massachusetts Ave., N.W., Washington, D. C.   20005.

Woman's Missionary Union, Southern Baptist Convention, 600 N. 20th St., Birmingham, Alabama   35203.

For most churches, denominational agencies related to ministry programs will be their primary resource. Other organizations and institutions should not be overlooked. The community agencies listed in Appendix A can help in many activities geared to meeting human need. Colleges, universities, and seminaries have departments which deal with ministry and which train persons for specific helping tasks. Faculty and students can be valuable resources to a church.

APPENDIX A

Community Resources

Not all communities will have each of the following resources. Some cities will have more; space is provided at the end to add other agencies, such as those sponsored by religious groups. But this list can serve as a basic guide to community resources. Fill in the address and telephone number for your area so that you will have them when needed.

Persons or Agency	Name of Contact Person	Address	Telephone
Alcoholics Anonymous			
Big Brothers of America			
Child Guidance Clinic			
Child Welfare Department			
College or Universities (Especially the departments of sociology, social work, education, and psychology)			
Community Welfare Council			
Council of Churches			
Denominational Office (Local)			
Domestic Relations Court			
Employment Services Public Private			
Family Service Association			
Goodwill Industries			
Home Demonstration Agent— United States Department of Agriculture			

Persons or Agency	Name of Contact Person	Address	Telephone
Homes for the Aged			
Hospitals			
Inner-City Mission Centers			
Institutions for the Retarded			
Job Corps Regional Office			
Judges, Attorneys			
Juvenile Authority			
Legal Aid Society			
Mental Health Association			
Mental Health Clinic			
Mental Hospitals			
Nursing Homes			
Office of Economic Opportunity			
Old-Age Assistance			
Parole and Probation Officers			
Planned Parenthood Association			
Police Narcotics Division Vice Division Juvenile or Youth Division			
Psychiatrists			
Psychologists			
Public Health Service			

Persons or Agency	Name of Contact Person	Address	Telephone
Public Housing			

Public Schools
   Guidance Department
   Special Education
     Department			

Public Welfare Department			
Red Cross			
Rescue Missions			
Salvation Army			
School for the Blind			
School for the Deaf			
Social Security Administration			
Traveler's Aid Society			
United Fund			
Unwed Mothers Homes			
Veterans' Administration			
Vocational Rehabilitation			
Volunteers of America			
YMCA			
YWCA			
Other:			

APPENDIX B

Resources for Referral

Complete this sheet and keep it available as a resource list for making referrals.

Need	Person or Agency for Referral	Address	Telephone
Aged			
Alcoholic			
Bereaved			
Birth Control			
Blind			
Childless Couple			
Compulsive Gambler			
Conscientious Objector			
Crippled			
Deaf			
Divorcee			
Drug Abuser			
Emotionally Disturbed			
Exceptional Child			
Expectant Mother			
Family Crisis			
Financial Crisis			
Homeless			
Homosexual			

Need	Person or Agency for Referral	Address	Telephone
Housing Substandard			
Hungry			
International			
Juvenile Offender			
Lonely			
Marriage Conflict			
Mentally Ill			
Mentally Retarded			
Migrant Worker			
Military Personnel			
Narcotic Addict			
Neglected Children			
Non-English Speaking			
Nonreader			
Overweight			
Parents			
Poor			
Potential Suicide			
Prisoner			
Refugee			
Released Prisoner			
Retired			

Need	Person or Agency for Referral	Address	Telephone
Runaway Youth			
Sick			
Unable to Afford Medical Care			
Institutionalized			
School Dropout			
Slow Learner			
Speech Handicap			
Unemployed			
Unwed Parent			

CHRISTIAN SERVICE SURVEY

FIRST BAPTIST CHURCH
515 McCullough Street
226-0363
San Antonio, Texas 78215

Env. No. _____

Please supply, check or circle only the information which applies to you. In the sections marked EMPLOYMENT SCHEDULE and CHRISTIAN EDUCATION and on the back, circle the CODE which applies to you and, if called for, one number which reflects your personal response.

Mr. Mrs. Miss					
NAME:					Date of
(Last)	(First)	(Middle)	Nickname or Name Preferred:	If married woman, Maiden Name:	Birth: ___/___/___ Mo. Day Yr.

PRESENT ADDRESS:

PERMANENT ADDRESS (If other than Present): Someone Who Will Always Know Your Address:

Street, Box, Rt.: _____ Street, Box, Rt.: _____ Name: _____ Relationship: _____

City, State: _____ City, State: _____ Street, Box, Rt.: _____

ZIP: _____ Phone: _____ ZIP: _____ Phone: _____ Area Code: _____ City, State, ZIP: _____

CHURCH MEMBERSHIP: Date Joined ___/___/___ Mo. Day Yr. Joined by Baptism _____ Joined by Statement _____ Joined by Letter _____

Letter from: _____ Baptist Church.

Street, Box: _____ City: _____ State: _____ ZIP: _____

Date Baptized or Letter Received: ___/___/___ Mo. Day Yr.

BUSINESS INFORMATION: Firm: _____ Profession, Industry: _____

Position/Job Description: _____ St. Box: _____

City, State: _____ ZIP: _____ Phone: _____

Mail to Business? _____ Tither: _____ Sex: M___ / F___ Head of Household _____ Adult w/Independent Income? _____ Live in Apt.? _____

Marital Status: Single _____ Married _____ Widowed _____ Divorced _____ Separated _____

CURRENT SCHOOL INFORMATION **ALUMNUS INFORMATION** **OTHER FORMAL EDUCATION**

School Now Attending: _____ College/Univ.: _____ School: _____

City, State: _____ City, State: _____ City, State: _____

Classification/Year: _____ Years Completed: _____ Degree: _____ Years: _____ Degree: _____

Major: _____ Minor: _____ Major: _____ Minor: _____ Major: _____

FAMILY: If under 7th Grade, Name of Parent or Guardian with whom live: _____

Name/Names of Relatives in FBC: _____

Other Family Members living in S.A. but not Members of FBC:

Name: _____ Address: _____ Age Division: _____ Church Membership. Or Preference: _____

EMPLOYMENT SCHEDULE

To determine how and when the church can best meet your needs, circle the CODE of as many of the following possibilities as seem appropriate.

DO YOU WORK....	Code		Code		Code	WHICH DAY OFF?	Code
School hours	WSH	Work some Sundays?	WSS	Shut-In or Disabled?	WSD	Sunday?	WSU
Regular 8 to 5 days?	WSI	Working wife/mother?	WWM	Retired Employed?	WPO	Monday?	WMO
2nd Shift (afternoon—night)?	WTW	College wks?	WCA	Family?	WPO	Tuesday?	WTU
3rd Shift (after midnight)?	WAM	Military Away?	WMA	Have Half-Day Off?	WHD	Wednesday?	WWE
Irregular Shifts	WTS	Weekly out-of-town	WOW			Thursday?	WTH
Work Occasionally?	WWO	Travel Required?	WTR			Friday?	WFR
Work every Sunday?	WES	Self-employed?	WBE			Saturday?	WSA

Code table (right column):

CODE	CHRISTIAN EDUCATION, OFFICE WORK	Now Serving Here Served	Will Serve
E01	Member-S.S.: ( )	1	2
E02	Member-T.U.: ( )	1	2
E03	Teacher-Preschool	1	2
E04	Elementary	1	2
E05	Youth	1	2
E06	Adults	1	2
E07	Day Care/Child Develop.	1	2
E08	Director (Supt.)-S.S.	1	2
E09	Outreach Leader (A. Supt.)	1	2
E10	Dept. Secretary	1	2
E11	V.B.S. Worker	1	2
E12	Class officer	1	2
E13	T.U. Sponsor-Youth	1	2
E14	T.U. Leader-Elem.	1	2
E15	General Office Work	1	2
E16	Telephoning	1	2
E17	Typing	1	2
E18	Dictation	1	2
	VISITATION (Code V)		
VEP	Evangelistic Prospects	1	2
VBP	Baptist Prospects	1	2
VNM	New Church Member	1	2
VSE	Shut-Ins/Extension	1	2
VCR	Cradle Roll	1	2
VCT	Census Taking	1	2
	MUSIC MINISTRY (Code M)		
MCM	Choir Member	1	2
MC1	Soprano	1	2
MC2	Alto	1	2
MC3	Tenor	1	2
MC4	Bass	1	2
MC5	Soloist	1	2
MC6	Vocal Ensemble	1	2
M11	**INSTRUMENTALISTS:** Piano	1	2
M12	Organ	1	2
M13	Percussion	1	2
M14	Brass	1	2
M15	Woodwinds	1	2
M16	Strings	1	2
	CHOIR DIRECTOR		
MD1	Youth (grades 7-8)	1	2
MD2	Youth (grades 9-12)	1	2
MD3	Elem. (grades 1-3)	1	2
MD4	Elem. (grades 4-6)	1	2
MD5	Preschool (ages 4-5)	1	2
MLD	SONG LEADER: Departmental	1	2
MLC	Congregational	1	2
MTV	MUSIC TEACHER: Voice	1	2
MTP	Piano	1	2
MTO	Organ	1	2
MSP	Sponsor-Elem. Choir	1	2
MSL	Music Secretary/Librarian	1	2
	GENERAL CHURCH SERVICE (Code G)		
GUS	Usher	1	2
GTR	Treasurer	1	2/___
GDE	Deacon	1	x
GLM	Licensed Minister	1	
GOM	Ordained Minister	1	
GJB	Junior Board	1	2
GCR	Vol. Church-Related Vacation	1	2

CHRISTIAN MINISTRIES — Using Skills and Interests in SERVICE

CODE S		Now Serving Have Served	Will Serve Train
S01	Speaking Spanish	1	2
S02	Medical Clinic asst.	1	2
S03	Well-Baby Clinic asst.	1	2
S04	Literacy	1	2
S05	Work w/ Internationals	1	2
S06	Work w/ Military	1	2
	Counseling for—		
S07	Elem. Day Camp	1	2
S08	Junior Camp/summer	1	2
S09	Youth Camp/retreat	1	2
S10	Youth Choir (tour)	1	2
	Transportation Skills—		
S11	Operator's License	1	2
S12	Commercial License	1	2
S13	Chauffeur's License	1	2
S14	First Aid/Camp Nursing	1	2
S15	Water Safety/Lifeguard	1	2
S16	Teach Citizenship/History	1	2
S17	Teach English	1	2
S18	Money Management/Consumer Education	1	2
	VOLUNTEERS for—		
S19	Intercessory through Office	1	2
S20	Office/phone	1	2
S21	Home visits	1	2
	Sunday: Sponsor for MbCH children		
S22	Homemaking skills—	1	2
S23	Sewing/Needlework	1	2
S24	Cooking/Nursing Hygiene/Health Educ.	1	2
S25	Tutoring	1	2
S26	Remedial Reading aid	1	2
S27	Clothing store/sorter	1	2
S28	Hospital volunteer	1	2
S29	Recreation w/Needy	1	2
S30	Child sitting for Needy	1	2
S31	Child Develop. Center	1	2
	Free Trans.—		
S32	Emergency short-term	1	2
S33	Long-time	1	2
S34	Transportation for Needy	1	2
S35	Shoppers for aged	1	2
S36	Office work-missions	1	2
S37	Library work-missions	1	2
S38	Participation in Services— In Juvenile Detention	1	2
S39	In Rescue Mission	1	2
S40	Hospitals, clinics	1	2
S41	Mobile Chapel	1	2
S42	Teach Extens. Bible Class	1	2
	Interpreting to Silent		
S43	Civil Defense	1	2
S44	Friends for Retarded	1	2
S45	Friends for Day-Care	1	2
S46	Friends for Deaf-Dumb	1	2
S47	Friends for Juv. Offenders	1	2
S48	Work w/Alcoholics	1	2

MINISTRIES CONTINUED

CODE		Now/Have	Will
	Providing Scholarship/Financial Aid for—		
S49	Sponsorship at MbCH	1	2
S50	Camp fees for Needy	1	2
S51	Children in Day Care	1	2
S52	Projects for Missions	1	2
S53	Emergency Relief Fund	1	2
S54	Aid for Families of Prisoners, Parolees		2
S55	Work w/ Mentally Retarded	1	2
S56	Work w/ other Handicapped	1	2
S57	Work w/ Potential Suicides	1	2
S58	Work w/ Addicts	1	2
S59	Marital Counseling	1	2
S60	Family Life Counseling	1	2
S61	Editing/Writing	1	2
S62	Radio/TV/Public Address	1	2

PROFESSION, VOCATION, EXPERIENCE

		CODE P
HEALTH/MEDICINE		
	Nursing: RN	PN1
	Nursing: LVN	PN2
	Nursing: Practical/Aide	PN3
	Doctor: Gen. Practice	PD1
	Ped.	PD2
	Gyn.	PD3
	Eye	PD4
	E-E-N-T	PD5
	Orth.	PD6
	Int. Medicine	PD7
	Psychiatry/Psychology	PD8
	Dentist	PD9
	Dental Hygienist/Asst.	PDH
	Pharmacist	PPH
	Therapist: Physical	PT1
	Occupational	PT2
	Medical Records	PRC
EDUCATION		
	Level: Kindergarten	PE1
	Elementary	PE2
	Secondary	PE3
	College/above	PE4
	Special Educ.	PE5
	Field: Teaching	PET
	Administration	PEA
	Counseling	PEC
CONSTRUCTION		
	Carpentry	PCC
	Plumbing	PCP
	Electrical	PCE
	Painting	PCT
	Roofing	PCB
	Bldg. Materials	PCM
	Masonry/Concrete	PCA
	Architect/Contractor	PCA
	Landscaping/Nursery	PCL
	Interior Design	PCI

VOCATIONS continued

CODE	BUSINESS/FINANCE/LAW		CODE	PUBLIC SERVICE
	Banking: Officer		PB1	Govt.: City
	Clerical		PB2	State
	Attorney/Legal Counsel		PB3	Federal
	Insurance		PB4	Services: Military
	Accounting		PB5	Postal
	Advertising/Public Rel.		PB6	Judicial/Law Enforce.
	Personnel		PB7	Utilities
	Secretarial		PB8	Fire Fighting
	SERVICES: Barber/Beauty	PPC	PSL	Maintenance
	Cleaning/Laundry	PPS	PSX	COMMUNICATIONS: Radio/TV
	Extermination	PPN	PST	Telephone
	Mechanics	PPM	PSM	Newspaper
	Tailoring/Sewing	PPP	PSG	SCIENCES: Mathematics
	Restaurant/Food Service	PPU		Physical/Earth
	Grocery/Bakery	PPJ	PSC	Space/Meteorolog.
	Retail Sales	PPU	PSE	Social/Political
	Contract Services	PPR	PSR	ARTS
	Real Estate	PC1, PC2, PC3	PAR	AGRICULTURE
	Rentals	PS1, PS2, PS3, PS4	PAG	

RECREATION

CODE R	RECREATION	Now Partici-pating	Interest in Parti-cipating	Interest in Coaching
	Sport Activities			
RSG	Golf	1	2	3
RSS	Softball-Baseball	1	2	3
RSF	Football	1	2	3
RSV	Volleyball	1	2	3
RST	Tennis	1	2	3
RSB	Basketball	1	2	3
	Camping			
RCF	Family camping	1	2	3
RCH	Hunting	1	2	3
RCR	Fishing	1	2	3
RCN	Nature study	1	2	3
	Hobbies			
RHC	Ceramics	1	2	3
RHO	Oil painting/drawing	1	2	3
RHA	Poster art	1	2	3
RHP	Photography	1	2	3
RHF	Flower arranging	1	2	3
RHD	Dramatics (all areas)	1	2	3
RHG	Gardening/Landscaping	1	2	3
RHI	Interior Decoration	1	2	3
RHX	Collecting	1	2	3
RHM	Metalcraft	1	2	3
RHL	Leathercraft	1	2	3
RHB	Basketry	1	2	3
	Social Activities/Fellowship			
RFS	Senior Adult Club	1	2	3
RFP	Picnics	1	2	3
RFA	All-church parties	1	2	3
RFB	Banquets	1	2	3
RFE	Performing entertainer	1	2	3
	Service Activities/Clubs			
RCS	Scouting	1	2	3
RCC	Civic Clubs	1	2	3
RCU	Cultural clubs	1	2	3
RC3	Boys/Girls Clubs	1	2	3

Standing Church Committees

Code C	Standing Church Committees	Now Serving Have Served	Will Serve
CAF	Armed Forces		2
CAU	Auditing		2
CAV	Audio-Visual Aids		2
CBA	Baptism		2
CBE	Benevolence		2
CBP	Building/Properties		2
CED	Education		2
CFE	Fellowship		2
CFF	Finance		2
CGR	Greeting		2
CHI	History		2
CKF	Kitchen/Food Service		2
CLI	Library		2
CLR	Long Range Planning		2
CLS	Lord's Supper		2
CMB	Membership		2
CMI	Mission		2
CMU	Music		2
CPK	Parking		2
CRC	Recreation		2
CSB	Social/Beautification		2
CST	Stewardship		2
CRT	Radio/TV/Communications		2
CTR	Transportation		2
CTU	Trustees		2
CVI	Visitation		2
CWT	WMU/Truth		2

Missionary Organizations

OBM	Baptist Men-Member		2
OMO	Baptist Men-Officer		2
OBW	Baptist Women-Member		2
OWO	Baptist Women-Officer		2
OAM	Acteens(YWA)-Member		2
OAL	Acteens-Leader		2
OGA	G.A.-Member		2
OGL	G.A.-Leader		2
ORA	R.A.-Member		2
ORL	R.A.-Leader		2
OMF	Mission Friends-Member		2
OML	Mission Friends-Leader		2

BLOOD TYPES (By circling choice 3, you are not obligating yourself to give blood.)

Code B		Will Give	Can't Give	Records Only
BOT	Type A	1	2	3
BO2	Type A Negative	1	2	3
BO3	Type AB	1	2	3
BO4	Type AB Negative	1	2	3
BO5	Type O	1	2	3
BO6	Type O Negative	1	2	3
BO7	Type B	1	2	3
BO8	Type B Negative / Don't Know Type	1	2	3